I have fought a good fight,

I have finished my course,

I have kept the faith.

TIMOTHY II 4:7

...les through" when he comes to
- when the bridge is
just has to swim
across. Our lads in
few days have done
of that kind of thing
site of the obstacles, they
on - killing & capturing they
are sure a good
fighting men.
According to our Army
paper. I see Milit Hep.
again leader of Ont Liberals.
suly they must be hard-up,
en they have to call him
t into office. Looks as
a spot on

BY AIR MAIL

AIR LETTER

IF ANYTHING IS ENCLOSED
THIS LETTER WILL BE SENT
BY ORDINARY MAIL.

Mrs D.P. ROWLAND,
1761 PRINCE EDWARD AVE.,
NIAGARA FALLS, ONT.,
CANADA.

Army Form W.307

THE
PADRE

BY AIR M

AIR LETTER

IF ANYTHING IS ENCLOSED
THIS LETTER WILL BE SENT
BY ORDINARY MAIL.

Army Form W.3424

OPENED

POSTAGE REVENUE

3D

PASSED BY
CENSOR
No
8105

MRS D. P. ROWLAND
1761 PRINCE EDWARD A
NIAGARA FALLS, ONT,
CANADA

D810
C36C3
2ea)

Army Form W.3077.

Barry D. Rowland

Amethyst

First printing November 1982.   Printed and bound in Canada

All rights reserved. The Padre © copyright 1982 by CAC, Inc.,
Published by Consolidated Amethyst Communications Incorporated
Unit #6, 60 Barbados Blvd., Scarborough, Ontario M1J 1K9 Canada

---

*The publisher gratefully acknowledges
the assistance of the Ontario Arts Council.*

Canadian Cataloguing in Publication Data
Rowland, David Parsons, 1908-1965.
The Padre
Correspondence of David Parsons Rowland.
Includes index.

ISBN 0-920474-25-X
1. Rowland, David Parsons, 1908-1965. 2. Chaplains,
Military – Presbyterian Church – Correspondence.
3. Chaplains, Military – Canada – Correspondence.
4. World War, 1939-1945 – Personal narratives, Canadian.
I. Rowland, B. D. (Barry D.), 1941–   II. Title.
D810.C36C3   940.54'78   C82-095180-3

Contents

This book is dedicated to the men of the Irish Regiment of Canada who served their country so valiantly in the days of war; to those of the Regiment who paid the supreme sacrifice in the pursuit of peace; to the families who kept the faith and lived within the shadow of fear and anxiety for so many years; to my mother whose love and dedication was without equal.

What had been the beautiful city of Arnhem was completely devastated at the time Canadian soldiers arrived in 1944.

Preface

As the storm clouds of war gather, nations are torn asunder, communities are devastated, families are fractured. The lives of men and women suffer irreparable damage.

This generation has not lived through a major conflict. The more removed we become, the more apt we are to view the sacrifice of many as distant ... we tend to take it for granted. The reasons for becoming committed to cause is lost on a generation who by and large *'dwell in a land of security.'* The irony, of course, is found in the hope of those who left family, friends and country to engage an enemy that threatened the peace and freedom of the world. It was the hope, yes the goal, of our fathers to set upon a course that would ensure that their sons and the children for generations to come, might never again sharpen the tools of war in order to defend the survival of entire nations. It is in this achievement that the extent of their sacrifice is minimized. November 11th somehow becomes a day when old soldiers parade, wear their medals, honour their fallen comrades. It is their remembrance not ours. We have become a nation of *'good-time Charlies.'* A people who have neither the time nor the inclination to reflect upon and practise the values of dedication, courage, commitment, concern. We are only too eager to dabble in shades of gray. To take a stand, to live by principles is not popular.

Someone once said that in times of catastrophe the strength of a nation is measured. Ordinary men and women rise from the ashes, dedicating their lives to the ideals that make nations strong. By their example, others are influenced to take up the torch to light the way through the darkness. From 1939-1945 the youth of this nation answered the call to war. It was clearly a matter of national survival. The reasons for going were many. They went to do something worthwhile; they went because they were lured by the excitement of war; they went because it was the thing to do; they went because it mean't you were a somebody; they went to fight a war and serve humanity.

Those very values that once seemed so remote became a reality, a way of life: dedication to a cause, concern for your comrade, commitment to an objective, courage in the face of adversity – these were the things that counted for they literally mean't survival. When a man knows fear and death and faces both on a daily basis, it is not easy to be strong. Ofttimes it is by example that one learns to maintain and shape one's character. Many a soldier can look back to an individual whose actions under the most trying of conditions was consistent to the point of being influential. Men rallied around him, felt safe in his presence, felt strength by his example, felt a sense of assurance in his honesty and courage.

One such man was Major the Reverend D.P. Rowland M.C. C.D.D.D. the Padre of the Irish Regiment of Canada.

The story that will unfold is a collection of remembrances of the Padre and of the men of the Irish Regiment. Thirty-seven years have passed since the bloody conflict yet it is very clear that men's lives have been dramatically influenced by the life and witness of the Padre. The measure of a man must surely be taken by the way he lives his life ... the way a man practises what he preaches. To be an effective leader of men you must have the courage of your convictions, respect and compassion for those around you, strength of personal character, unshakable faith in your principles. The Padre epitomized all of these. These recollections are straightforward and moving.

Would that each of us in our lifetime could leave such an indelible mark on our fellowman.

David Parsons Rowland

DAVID PARSONS ROWLAND was born in Dublin, Ireland on September 23, 1908. One of a family of ten brothers and sisters, he emigrated to Canada as a young man, continued his education while at the same time engaging in a variety of manual occupations. During this time he heard the call to the Christian ministry and enrolled at Knox College in Toronto, where he graduated and was ordained into the ministry of the Presbyterian Church of Canada in 1935. While attending college he was greatly interested in athletics and played for the University of Toronto and Knox College soccer teams. He held the highest honours that the University of Toronto and Knox College could confer on any athlete. While still a student at college, he organized the congregation at York in the west end of Toronto in 1934 and was called and inducted as its first minister on June 8, 1936. He continued in that service until his death in the summer of 1965.

In 1938 the first phase of the church building was opened and dedicated. When war broke out he resigned from his congregation to accept a commission as Chaplain of the Irish Regiment of Canada and went overseas and served with distinction during the conflict. He was decorated with the Military Cross and mentioned in despatches. When war ceased, he returned from active service and was again called by York Presbyterian Church. Through his suggestion the name of the church was changed to York Memorial Presbyterian Church as a tribute to Canada's war dead. Through his capable and zealous leadership the congregation grew rapidly and the church proper was completed and opened in 1952. His personal dedication to the youth of his community resulted in the opening and dedication of the Christian Education building which was named the David Parsons Rowland Youth Centre as a tribute to his excellent leadership and service. The same year, Knox College honoured him by conferring on him the degree of Doctor of Divinity, honoris causa.

Major Rowland continued to take a keen interest in the Irish Regiment and was Chaplain of the peace unit until the time of his death. He was also a leader in the fight against the government's decision to submerge the Militia Regiment in the National Defense reorganization. He was Chaplain of the Silverthorn Branch 57 of the Legion, the 36th Ulster Division Old Comrades Association. He was an active Orangeman and Past Provincial Grand Master of the Grand Lodge of Ontario West, Past Imperial Grand Chaplain of the Imperial Grand Lodge of the World, Vice-President of the St. Patrick's Irish Benevolent Association.

In community life, Dr. Rowland gave of himself in assisting people of all creeds and classes. Having served as Chairman of the Parole Board of

Ontario he was ever considerate of those who were in difficulty and the facilities of the Rowland Youth Centre were available as a community centre. Subsequent to the upheavel in York Township's municipal affairs, Dr. Rowland decided to run for municipal office and was elected Deputy Reeve where he served as an effective and well respected administrator and public representative for four years.

In the church at large he was much sought after as a preacher. He served on many boards and committees of the church. At the time of his death he was Chairman of the Chaplaincy Committee and also the Chaplaincy Committee of the Canadian Council of Churches. He was the first Moderator of the Presbytery of West Toronto.

Seldom has so great a tribute been paid to a minister of the gospel. At his funeral the church proper, the basement of the church, the Youth centre and the grounds around were filled beyond capacity. A public address system had to be installed so that the service could be heard by all. In the Acts and Proceedings of the Ninety-Second General Assembly of the Presbyterian Church in Canada the tribute was best stated:

'Wherever his work took him, he was always devoted to the cause of Christ whether on the playing field, the battlefield, in the fraternal lodge, the council chamber, the congregation or the church at large. He enlisted the lives and services of men and women in the work of the Kingdom. Multitudes of people can testify that he was behind many of the good things that happened to them. He was an ardent Christian, a wise counsellor, a loyal friend and a kindly pastor.'

Following is the Citation accompanying the decoration of Honourary Major Rowland with The Military Cross by His Majesty King George VI:

This Chaplain has served with The Irish Regiment of Canada since June 1940. During the years of training in Canada and afterwards in Britain he did excellent work in maintaining the state of high morale by his contributions in the recreational and educational field. His contacts with the men in matters of spiritual welfare have been of the best, and his understanding and sympathetic help have earned the appreciation of all ranks. During the Hitler Line Campaign and the attack on the Gothic Line he was of the greatest assistance to the Unit Medical Officer, working unceasingly as long as there was a casualty in the post. Although under constant mortar and small arms fire, this gallant Officer worked from the Regimental Aid Post to the Forward Companies, rendering first aid and personally assisting in the evacuation of the wounded. Honourary Captain Rowland has won the sincere admiration and confidence of the men by showing, as a non-combatant, the desire to share their danger, and his presence has helped greatly to rally the shaken. After the Battle he has worked without rest to assure that the soldiers killed in action should have a reverent and prompt burial. This Chaplain by his devotion to duty, skill and energy in comforting the wounded, and steadiness under heavy shell fire has encouraged and strengthened all ranks, and has set an example most worthy of recognition.

POSTAGE REVENUE

Mrs D.P. Rowland
1161 PRINCE EDWARD Ave,

PASSED BY
CENSOR

better, do an extra fine job
on it. She was doing my e
today and what do you know
she thinks I have a little
the devil in them. when b
told her thats how I wore
married my wife. I thoug
she would split her sides
of bad, my darling. I'm sen
it when finished home to
a little laugh at my ex/
will do your heart goo

This afternoon I was an
football. The way I feel
know I must be get
be a very old man.
Ink, he any use to you
I get back? Anyway
~ that made the lads
team very happy.
darling, daily I'm
and Barny, me
my aut

Memoirs from the Front

Correspondence with loved ones was the soldier's lifeline. It kept him in touch with a world that was, for the most part, orderly and predictable, where strategies for keeping alive from day to day were not part of the ordinary routine. Everyday happenings were of the utmost importance to him: the little boy growing up, the family gatherings, the holiday at the summer cottage, the spring walks, the summer picnics – these became the foundation of a man's strength enhancing his determination to carry on.

Many words and expressions of fear, loneliness, honesty, truth, wonderment, were written and read over and over again in muddy slit trenches or pup tents pitched on rain drenched foreign soil. The censor could clip the words but he could not destroy the sentiment and feeling.

It is important to remember that this was a time when young men were coming face to face with experiences that were very new to them. They travelled through countries that previously were mere names in history books. They were mixing with civilians whose lives, families and homes had been torn apart by war. As they moved from battlefield to battlefield they saw their comrades and friends killed and wounded in a most horrible fashion. In the course of their duty they were required to kill other human beings. Young men who were witnessing the human condition at its worst.

The Padre wrote home to his family ... over five hundred letters. He also kept a personal diary throughout the war. His thoughts form a unique account of the days of war as seen through the eyes of a Christian Padre as he carried out his duties and responsibilities. The pages that follow touch on many events, from the ordinary to the tension filled days of front-line fighting. It is one man's personal reflections ... a non-combatant who won the sincere admiration and confidence of the men by showing the desire to share their danger at every turn. His recollections are flavoured with a spectrum of emotions ... humour, sadness, anger, love, wonder, futility, exhilaration, pride, humility.

Not only will his accounts stir the memory of those who served in one particular regiment but all soldiers who have lived the daily routine of war.

Over the Pond and on to England

November 4, 1942.

Things have been going very well and we have all enjoyed the trip so far. The meals have been perfectly wonderful. We only get two a day so one tends to eat enough at breakfast at 10:30 a.m. to last until supper at 8:00 p.m. Nobody seems to be seasick, in fact the ship is much better than the train that got us to dockside. The men are thoroughly excited about the whole thing and they haven't uttered a complaint. They are well-fed and well-bunked so that adds greatly to their good humour. I conducted my first service on board ship and was more than pleased that the place was packed. Everything looks interesting from where I stand. To say that we have travelled without incident would be putting it all in perspective. We will soon be at our destination. Thank God for the safe trip!

November 6, 1942.

We've now arrived in Dear Old England! It has taken us just a week from the time we left Canada to arrive at our destination. Not bad going in wartime. We left the ship in good order on Thursday and boarded the train. We saw a lot of very wonderful country as well as many strange sights. The lay out of the towns, cities and houses are quite different to anything we have in Canada. Actually, much of it reminded me of my early days in Ireland. During the train ride I had the opportunity to talk with many people. They seem to be taking things in a calm matter-of-fact manner. Some of them have been bombed out and have lost loved ones, yet they have high hopes and a firm belief that the enemy will soon be licked.

We rolled into our camp at three in the morning. Everything was blacked out and of course there was a good healthy rain falling. We got the men settled, had something to eat and were in bed by 6:00 a.m. It is difficult to get a handle on the place as yet since all our time is being spent getting things in order. Six of us are housed in a cottage called '*York*' (minus Presbyterian) that is heated by small fireplaces. Since coal is limited I really don't know how we will make out. The place is comfortable and that's all that matters. The meals so far have been acceptable and although we don't get quantity, the quality is first rate. It won't be long before we get everything in shape and we will soon be off to see a few places and sights. Apparently I get seven days leave anytime I want it but I'll wait until Christmas and head off to Ireland. That should be a grand spot for Christmas dinner!

November 11, 1942.

We are finally settled in. Last evening I went downtown for a walk but the blackout made things seem very strange so I soon headed back to camp. With daylight I finally had the opportunity to see the town and locate the sights. The first article one must purchase is a map since you just can't manage without one. It is quite an attractive town and the people are very kind and most civil. Everywhere one looks – behind stores, in front of homes, at bus stations – one sees air raid shelters constructed. There seems no chance that the people will be caught unprepared. Everyone has great assurance that it will soon be over. During the week I attended my first chaplains' meeting at which we lined up our work for the week. I also visited the Canadian Soldiers' Club and attended a so-so stage show at the Hippodrome.

November 15, 1942.

We were up very early this morning and had a Brigadier's Regimental Inspection. The inspection used up most of the morning and our men put on a great display that seemed to please the Brigadier. I must say that it does get cold standing around a parade ground. After we dispersed, I joined a few of the lads and went to see my first professional soccer game in England. Aldershot was playing Crystal City. It was a wonderful game with players on both teams displaying fine ball control. I would like to play like some of them ... guess I'm too old now to even start. I shall be seeing plenty of games while here since it's a good way to put in an afternoon.

I have been spending a great deal of time preparing my sermon for Sunday morning. We're paying 10 shillings for the use of an Anglican church. Preaching from an Anglican church in England is a real achievement for a Presbyterian! I'm sure the men will appreciate the opportunity to worship in a church for a change rather than a barracks.

The news is more encouraging everyday. The sooner we lick the Nazi the better! It's difficult to imagine that a war is going on where we are located, although you see many soldiers – men and women alike – in uniform. There really seems to be no one left for civilian occupations. Everyone seems cheery and bright about the whole thing. They certainly make the Canadian soldier feel at home.

November 18, 1942.

I caught the train this morning for my first visit to London. I arrived at Waterloo Station and took a taxi to the Canadian Officers' Club. At the door a lady ahead of me dropped her glove and naturally, being a gentleman, I picked it up. She introduced herself as Mrs. Vincent Massey, the High Commissioner's wife. She runs the club for Canadian officers. She is a very busy woman and is doing an excellent job on our behalf.

As soon as I left the club I walked along Regent Street to Oxford then to Marble Arch and down to Hyde Park. I entered through the gates at Constitutional Hill and soon found myself in front of Buckingham Palace. You can't get in but I did go up and put my hands on the gate knobs – thought it might be lucky. From there I walked on to Trafalgar Square and on to Whitehall where the government houses are located. I stopped and had a good look at 10 Downing Street. Who should come out but Mrs. Roosevelt (she's quite a busy woman right now). I soon continued on to Westminster Abbey, Scotland Yard and the Houses of Parliament. I moved on to the Rendevous Club for afternoon tea and then headed along the Strand to St. Paul's Cathedral. What a magnificentsight! All around it buildings had been flattened yet it stands as if to say, "You can do us no harm". You can see that my first day in London was a busy one.

One of my roles is to take on the duties of the educational officer of the Unit. The program appears to have merit and should prove an asset to the men as it will give them something to occupy their time. Since I have a corporal for my assistant, I likely will be able to share the load. I also organize the soccer practices for our team. They have excellent playing fields here – a real treat after the 'sands of Debert'. My other duties at present involve visitations to the hospitals, where some of the lads have been admitted with severe colds, and a few personal interviews with the men. Our set up to date looks like a good show.

November 25, 1942.

Here it is the end of another week. Today was generally a light one. I spent about an hour in the office and then walked over to visit four of our lads in hospital. I spent some time on the educational programs. The men are going for it in a big way. It takes some time to find out what each man is best suited for. One lad wanted to know if there was a course on "How To Make Your Wife Love You"; another inquired about 'Ballroom Dancing' – apparently one needs to know this to get along over here. I spent the evening with a Mr. Buckley, the auxiliary service man from the Y.M.C.A. He arranges for the men to go on leave. It's wonderful how this country has received our boys.

It's about a month ago that we waved goodbye to Halifax. Time seems to go by very quickly around here. It's most encouraging to read the papers these days for it really looks like we are beginning to roll up the Nazi carpet. So much happens in one day, one never knows how much will be accomplished in a few months. Many feel that the whole thing will be over in a year. Maybe they are too optimistic but I pray that they are right.

November 28, 1942.

I had a great night's sleep but a lousy breakfast. I'm afraid the cook overslept. We had sausages and potatoes but they were cold. We are messing with the 15th Field Artillery and with so many in the mess it's getting difficult to feed us all. We hope to get into our own mess next week and that should prove to be a better arrangement.

We had our first Regimental football practice in preparation for our first game. The ground was soft and consequently I was mud up to my neck. Whatever our strategy it paid off as we won the game 9-0. Everybody on the team seemed to get a goal – got one myself. I certainly enjoy the game and it's great exercise and that seems to be the order of the day over here. I never saw our men go through so much P.T. Everyday each company has to go through a cross-country run of 5-10 miles. The training is most intensive but the men are responding extremely well.

Time is moving on and so is the war. I read in the paper about the outcome of the French fleet. The Germans are slowing up. They are missing tricks at more places than Toulouse. Their plans for the French seem to have backfired. Anyday I expect to hear that they can't find Hitler!

We have been most fortunate with the weather since we arrived in England. As I walked along to church on Sunday I noticed flowers still in bloom in some gardens. The frost which is light here, apparently hasn't caught up with them. We had a fine service and the men were most receptive throughout.

As I headed back to my quarters I couldn't help but feel a little homesick. 'Tis a strange and cruel world we live in where distance is becoming a kind of tyrant. We say that the world is getting smaller but that's a fallacy when we must be so far away from our loved ones.

December 1, 1942.

Here it is the first day of December. It won't be long before Christmas is upon us. It is going to be very tough not to be home with our families. I'm getting ready for my first trip back to Ireland and I'm wondering what kind of a reception I'll get when my feet touch the old sod. I have a few things to do before setting out. The C.O. is sending 12 lads up for officer courses so I have to go over the educational programs involved. I also have to spend time with the men on a battleschool course. It's really a thorough one – climbing mountains, jumping ditches, scaling walls. The training will make the men tough and fit for combat.

We were informed today that all padres over 45 would be taken out of active units and sent to hospital and holding units. It affects six or seven of our group. I don't like the idea myself but I suppose those in authority know what they are doing.

Back to the Old Sod

December 12, 1942.

My leave to Ireland began on December 2. Bob Rowland and I were up bright and early and Paul Russell, my batman, drove us to the station where we took the early train to London. We had a three hour wait but put in the time sight-seeing around the city. After a lengthy train ride we arrived at the point of embarkation, had a good supper and went to bed. We awoke at dockside in Belfast harbour.

It was very dark when we came down the gangplank but to put my feet on Irish soil again after an absence of twenty years was a real thrill. We jumped into a horse and cab and headed for the station. On the way we were reminded, as we saw many bombed out buildings, that the German had also paid a visit here. Just as in England, the people were going about their jobs as if nothing had happened. We caught the train and headed for Portadown. It took us about an hour to make the trip and all along the way I kept looking for places and things that would remind me of my youth.

When we arrived in Portadown, Bob and I parted company and I hailed a cab and headed out to visit neighbours whom we lived beside in the early days. The Coulters gave me a great welcome and I wasn't in the house very long before they sat me down to a good meal of ham and eggs. What a treat and a surprise for I hadn't had a fresh egg since I left Canada! To say I enjoyed it is putting it mildly! In the afternoon I took a bike into Portadown where I looked over the shops and people I knew so many years ago. There didn't seem to be much change except for a few houses. On the way back I stopped at the old house. I had many recollections flashing through my mind. I thought of the days when we were all kids playing around together. Across the road was an old orchard where many times I stole apples. I'm sure Mother would have given much to be on hand. In the evening I attended a church social in the old schoolhouse. There were many there I knew, but like me they had grown old. As I went from room to room, the days of my youth came flowing back. I could hear the voice of the teacher calling me out to lay the cane across my poor hands! I could feel its sting as if it happened yesterday. I looked up in the school register to see what kind of pupil I was. This is what it said: 'good in his work, bad in his conduct'. A little humiliating, but it was a grand night and I left with a feeling that it was good for me to have been there.

On Friday, I changed into civilian clothes and caught the train for Dublin. I met Bob a few stops ahead and we spent the time in great discussion until we pulled into Dublin Station. After getting settled into a hotel, I began to make my rounds. Dublin is a fine city with many historical settings. I went to my uncle's in the afternoon and they were most pleased to see me. Since they have six children working at various occupations, I had to wait until midnight before I saw them all. I could have listened to them talk for days! They had such beautiful accents, much softer than one hears in the north. It was a most entertaining and interesting evening.

In the morning I caught the train for Sligo. Since there is a shortage of coal in this part of the country, they burned turf or peet in the engine. It was the longest train ride I ever had ... it took us nine hours to travel about 100 miles. My uncle met me at the train and took me home. They have a beautiful spot, attached to an old Irish estate on a lake that boasts fine hunting and fishing. I spent a few hours walking around the woods and seeing some of the ancient land marks.

I returned to Portadown on Monday and after a good night's sleep I awoke early on Tuesday, took a bike and rode to a place called Lurgan. It brought back some vivid memories as I biked along the country roads over which I travelled as a boy. Each house I passed would conjure up a memory that would bring a smile to my face. One dear lady that I used to visit and run messages for was so thrilled to see me that she kissed me and remarked that of all the Rowlands who might have become a minister, I was the last one she would pick. When she recalled some of the things that I did I could understand why she was so amazed. Ah, sometimes I feel undone and very humble!

On Wednesday it was raining very hard so I had to stay in until the late afternoon. After the rain I went to visit my brother's grave in Seago. It seemed strange to stand beside it and recall some twenty-one years ago when we laid him to rest there. I have ordered a little plaque to be placed on it.

All good things must come to an end. I caught the train for Belfast on Friday morning and was soon back in England. When I arrived back at camp, everything was very much the same as when I left.

Still in England

December 19, 1942.

We've had a rather lack lustre week ... damp and unseasonably mild for December. One is reminded of good old wet and sloppy Debert. I haven't been bothering with breakfast (one can miss this meal over here and be none the worst for it) but still Paul has been getting me up bright and early. I think sometimes that he has trouble sleeping and can't bear to see me enjoying mine. He does make a great cup of tea and it does hit the spot.

Most of the week has been spent organizing the educational programs. I'm suppose to have a corporal assigned to help me but so far he has not arrived. The men are taking to it reasonably well and if they continue to be serious, it will prove a great help when the time comes to re-establish themselves. I started 20 men on typing and shorthand courses. The instruction was so excellent that I sat in on the sessions myself and I think I will continue to do so.

I spent several hours at the hospitals visiting the men. We have about a dozen lads suffering from the flu. They certainly look after them wonderfully well; I haven't received a complaint. They all seem to be in good spirits particularly the ones for whom I have parcels and mail from home.

The 'C' company lads held a dance in the Dominion Soldiers' Club on Friday night. Bill Elder was anxious that I go since he was the only officer with his lads. The boys had a terrific time and behaved beyond expectations. The lady in charge told us that they were by far, the best bunch of lads she had ever entertained. I just hope they continue in this direction.

December 25, 1942.

Christmas Day h.. arrived – our first in England. The first thing I did was to go to church after which I came back to the mess to help pu. ......shing touches on our arrangements for the day. We have the mess well decorated with a very beautiful Christmas tree right in the centre. The men paraded in to '*Hark the Herald Angels Sing*' played over our public address system. They just got nicely into their first course when in came the General. The boys gave him a loud Irish welcome and he left to the strains of '*For He's a Jolly Good Fellow*'. The Colonel, followed by the company commanders, gave brief greetings. This was the best Christmas we have had in the Unit (it has been our third).

I spent the afternoon in the hospital playing Santa to our lads. I must say it is still a very lonely time as we are so mindful of o'r families back home. We know that it won't always be like this and that's what keeps our spirits high.

December 26, 1942.

Today is Boxing Day. Everyone has a holiday except the Canadian troops. I started the day with a good cup of tea. I'm getting more spoiled with each day ... it sure will be tough in civilian life. No one was too ambitious today, although we had a Regimental parade for the c.o. that lasted for about half an hour.

I'm trying out a new scheme: a noon broadcast for the men. I play a few records, give a short resume of the news, a little more music, the Regimental news. I think we're going to have some fun with it. This afternoon I spent time preparing my sermon for Sunday '*Resolutions for the Coming Year*'.

One of the lads got word that his wife was critically ill with pneumonia and was in the hospital. I felt so sorry for him when he got the news; he just wanted to get back right away. We have no choice but to wait and hope for the best.

December 29, 1942.

Last Sunday I brought my New Year's message to the men and from all indications it was well received. That evening we had a show in the mess but it was so cold that we had to keep our coats on throughout. One fireplace is hardly big enough to keep us all warm so we took turns at the grate.

My noon broadcasts are proceeding reasonably well although frankly I'll be glad when the Russians get the Germans out of their country since I'm having a time pronouncing some of their cities. If any interesting news comes in from Canada through the mail of some of the men, that too gets a place and receives a warm reception.

Most of my evenings were spent writing a few letters and cleaning up the batmen in cribbage. Some nights I can't get licked; some nights I can't win a hand.

At the chaplains' meeting this morning I learned that I was to go with my Unit to the 5th Division. I'm very pleased that I can stay with my own Unit and have been considered good enough to remain with the Irish.

December 31, 1942.

There is just one more day left in the old year. It seems strange that there is not more winter over here although this morning when I drew back my blackout curtains, the first thing to greet my eyes was snow! I thought I was back in Canada but it only lasted for about an hour.

My noon broadcasts are taking some time to prepare. The news looks good and we all hope the Russians keep on moving the Germans back. The Eighth Army is also making great progress. It looks like we have Hitler on the run. It must be a bitter pill for him to take; he's been pushing us around for so long it's nice to feel the shoe is on the other foot. During the broadcast today one of the lads announced twins for one of the boys. Did he ever get a hand! They carried him all around the mess singing '*I Want to Go Home to Ma*'. My sentiments exactly.

We prepared a special dinner for the men. Some had girlfriends with them while those of us who were unattached sat down at a big table and had a heap of fun. We sang songs and made speeches ... some good, some not so good. After we rang in the New Year I returned to my room where Paul was sitting in bed with a cup of tea beside him. I asked him where mine was and he swung his hand to show me and promptly tipped his tea all over himself. I think I laughed till I was sore (I just couldn't help it). I got a good telling off but still managed to get my cup of tea. Before I turned in I wrote the following in my diary: '*Good-bye Old Year, you've been good to us in that you gave us the first small light of victory. You hurt us when you took us away from our loved ones but you whispered that it would not be for long. May Almighty God spare us and keep us strong in body and mind defending us against our enemies and in the New Year bring us peace*'.

January 1, 1943.

Happy New Year 1943! It is a very wet morning not at all like a New Year's day. This is a Canadian army holiday ... suppose the authorities feel we need it after the night before and I can assure you that for some it is a blessing. We had an air raid warning just after noon today but there was no action. The German planes are scarce now in England; they have lots to keep them going elsewhere. Our orchestra was on hand and gave the boys some peppy music. We sang songs and when we sang '*O Canada*' the boys nearly brought the roof down! They all seemed very happy and this noontime program seems to lift their spirits. About 1:00 p.m. all the officers marched over to the Brigade mess where we had our New Year's dinner. It was so long coming that we became very impatient. The meal was passable although the pudding didn't taste so hot.

January 8, 1943.

I had a lot of the lads in to see me this week with a variety of problems. Besides my interviews I spent several afternoons visiting the lads in hospital and delivering their mail and smokes. Although we have had some snow it rarely lasts for more than a couple of hours. We played football on Saturday afternoon, and with a strong second half we won the game 5-2. We haven't been licked yet but I'm pretty tired and have been nursing a few bruises since the game.

On Sunday, following my service, I caught the train for Oxford to visit with my uncle and his family. Oxford is a city of colleges and churches. The streets are very narrow and just seem to be 'pushed' together in a most irregular fashion. I had a very pleasant visit and thoroughly enjoyed the train ride back through the peace and beauty of the English countryside.

The dampness finally got to me and I spent Wednesday, Thursday and today in bed with a cold. Bill Elder, Bill Leonard and Lou Quitt dropped in to see how I was getting along. I think they think I'm 'swinging the lead'. I got up tonight and, Paul and I set about cleaning up and rearranging the room. It's wonderful what you can see needs changing when you look at it for a couple of days from bed.

January 10, 1943.

This was a beautiful Sunday morning, much like our May mornings back home. I had my first service at 9:00 a.m. and the church parade at 10:45 a.m. The men entered the service in fine fashion. I referred to building castles in the sand ... some on the lakes of Ontario, Superior, Huron, Simcoe. That brought a smile to many of their faces.

After dinner I had an interview with a soldier and his wife who had been separated for six years. It was a time for remending broken vows so I thought it appropriate to reread the marriage service to them. They left me feeling that it was all worthwhile and determined to make a better go of it this time. I felt something positive had been accomplished particularly since I have been working on the case for quite a few months.

January 14, 1943.

I held my first discussion group with 'B' company. It was quite interesting and the boys seem glad to have this kind of a change worked into their schedule. They are sure throwing some tough questions at me although many I have heard so often that an answer is not too difficult. One lad asked me, "Can you be a good Christian and not go to church?" I broke precedent a little and answered him with a question. "Can you be a good soldier and not be in the army or a good swimmer and not go into the water?" All in all they seemed most interested and we had a good session.

Since we have received orders for moving I paid my last visit to the boys in hospital in this part of the country. They were wondering what they would do for mail so I've made sure that they will be looked after and won't miss out. Mail is our life's blood in this country!

We were up bright and early today, boarded the train and eventually arrived at our destination. It almost took my breath away when I saw the place where we were to live. It's a castle and has all the trimmings. There are three of us in a large room that has central heating and a large bath. The grounds around the place are perfectly wonderful with gardens, trees and walkways. Shortly after arriving I spoke to another padre by phone. We are in the same Brigade which means one of us will have to go – no room for two Presbyterians in the same place! I told him that I didn't want to leave the Irish and he said that since he had been moved around so much he would like to stay put. I guess it will be up to the powers that be to make the decision.

January 30, 1943.

My sporting duties got me involved in arranging for a Brigade boxing school. We took over a house for the boxers, who like the idea of getting a couple of weeks off for solid training. Maybe, of course, they like boxing better than soldiering. I'll take the soldiering! I also spent time organizing the Brigade cross-country run. We are preparing for the Divisional run that comes up in February.

On Wednesday we had our Brigadier's inspection. We got started at 9:00 a.m. and didn't finish until 5:00 p.m. I was on the job throughout and got some pretty good pictures although it was a pretty poor day weather-wise.

Paul and I unpacked some fourteen parcels that came for men who are no longer in the Unit. Some left us before we came over; some have left us since. We can't send them back so I have set up a special food shelf in our hospital and when I find a man who needs something special I just give him an item from the shelf. Soups are the hardest things to come by and are the big items in demand. I have written to all the folks who sent the parcels and I do hope that they are satisfied with my scheme.

February 5, 1943.

Sunday was a real English day. It rained and blew until I thought Providence was preparing another Noah episode! I had a busy morning: first parade at 9:00 a.m.; second parade at 10:00 a.m.; third at 11:00 a.m. It was like old times going around the companies again. I do enjoy the smaller groups as I am able to get more across to them.

My educational corporal, a chap called Butler, from Stratford, has now arrived. I have lots of work for him to do. The other day I noticed that he was wearing an Orangeman's ring. Apparently it was given to him by a close friend and he liked the design. I started kidding him about what he would do when an Orangeman met him. He told me that several times men had met him, given him signs, and he didn't know what to do. He asked me if he should take it off and of course I told him to leave it where it was. He's a great kid and I like him a lot.

Today was a light day and since Bob Rowland had left on a 48 hour, I have taken over as paymaster. I hope I won't be short by the time he returns. We played the Perth today in soccer and lost 2-1. One of the padres was bad-mouthing me through the gate so I fixed him proper after the match. I got a bad leg out of it but should be fine in a couple of days.

February 13, 1943.

As I passed into church before the parade, I noticed spring flowers beginning to come up all around the grounds. I had two morning parades and spoke on the subject of prayer. Each evening at nine we are attempting to dedicate a minute to prayer. Many of the officers and men are observing it.

I have been busy making out chaplain reports. It's all in a days work and we have to do them each week. I'm afraid the authorities over here are getting too efficient. My educational work is going full steam ahead. We have about 60 men taking practical courses Sunday mornings at a nearby town. The soldier is getting a real opportunity in this war. Had some of us to pay for what we are now getting for free, it would run into a considerable sum. My discussion groups are going strong and the questions are getting tougher: "If Britain and Germany worship the same God why do we fight one another?" If the Bible says, 'Thou shalt not kill', is it right for me to kill a German?" They are putting some real thought into our sessions.

I had a lad in to see me whom I married in 1941. He had a letter from his wife telling him that she didn't love him anymore and had found someone else. He loves her very much and was very upset. I gave him the best advice that I could but it's a devil of a thing to happen with lives so young. Then, we are so far away and there is little that one can do in a hurry. We are getting a number of problems like this. I know that it can work both ways but that is little comfort to the one affected.

This morning I was up at six. I had a funeral for a young lad who belonged to the Army Service Corps. He was a Presbyterian, just eighteen and lived in Toronto. He was killed in a motorcycle accident. I had to go a long way for the service so I didn't return until quite late. I'm preparing to write his mother this evening. It is very sad to see young lads go out in such a way.

Lets Toughen Them Up

March 14, 1943.

I have just returned from a 16 day scheme. Let me fill you in on my doings.

In a little jeep packed to the hilt, Paul and I took our place in the convoy around 5:00 p.m. We drove through a very dark night made worse by a bit of rain. With no lights on, it made it difficult at times to stay on the road. We reached our first stopping off point at 5:00 a.m. and it didn't take long to pull out our bedding and get down to sleep. Fortunately we stopped in some woods where we had a bit of good shelter and proceeded to grab about five hours sleep. It was kind of odd sleeping outside but we were soon to learn that one can sleep anywhere when tired.

We were called at 10:00 a.m. the following day for breakfast. It didn't take me long to get going as I was hungry and under a grand sun with lots of warmth, packed into it. I ate until I was ashamed of myself. After breakfast I had a shave in a cup of warm water ... I never knew I could do so much in such a small utensil. It was afternoon before I knew it and I grabbed my bedroll and hid in the bushes for about two hours of "catch-up". We were on the road again around 8:00 p.m. The night was clear which helped a lot. These jeeps are cold; you catch every bit of wind that's going. We got into our next spot around 2:00 a.m. There was a lot of frost around so I found an old shed with a lean to and there I made my abode.

The call for breakfast came at 8:00 a.m. When I awoke and looked around I found we were situated in a beautiful piece of country. I took a long walk through a nearby woods. Everywhere the spring flowers were out in full bloom – primroses, violets, snowdrops – they just seemed to cover the place. While strolling I came upon a lovely home with a grand garden. Being a curious fellow, I went and knocked on the door. A very nice lady answered the door and consented to let me walk through her garden. She was delighted that I called and invited me in to have a bit of breakfast. After a feed of bacon and eggs, I saw the garden in a much better light and gave it a lot more praise as well! The lady's name was Mrs. Howard and her husband was President of Imperial Tobacco. They took me to Southhampton which was close by and for three days I was entertained in their home.

We moved again around 8:00 p.m. When I awoke in the morning I found myself on the grounds of a convent. I was just crawling out of my bedroll when a nun passed me. I'm sure I gave her quite a shock. It was comfortable through the night although sleeping in your clothes tends to make you feel very dirty. We were just settling down to dinner when the call came to move again. We didn't get a chance to eat until the next morning. It was a very long stretch and I think I was about as fed up as anyone.

On Thursday we just pulled in by the side of the road and I found a hay stack where Paul and I lay down, very tired. Despite the rats that were running around we had a good sleep. We ate our breakfast at the side of the road after which we retreated for a few miles and came to Lord Root's estate where we settled in for the day and night. I wonder how long this will keep up.

We moved again on Saturday morning. We passed through Hungerford, a nice town with many old houses and thatched roofs. We stopped for a while and the women of the town came out and served us tea. As we went along all the townsfolk came out and gave us big smiles. The children, as everywhere, crowded around us asking for badges. I had a lot of fun with them. We stopped near a place by the name of Lambourn. To our surprise we were right beside an Italian prisoner of war camp. Our friend Nick Vendetti had a big time with them. They were all very happy and were not very interested in the war. One lad said that he was better off as a prisoner than a soldier in Italy!

I had two services on Sunday. One with the Unit and the other with Cape Breton Highlanders. I was just in the middle of one when a call came for a move and the lads had to jump right out of the service and get going. It was like taking religion on the run! I managed a bath from a can filled with water. I feel cleaner now. George Duncan was called away and I was left in command of the company. I had quite a time and the boys got a great kick out of it. Fortunately everything went well, so I had no real worries.

We're on the move again. We're now getting used to moving anytime of the day or night. Last night I slept in a pigpen (without the pigs). Had there been any I'm sure they would have moved out. Today we passed through Gloucester, Cheltenham and Tewkesbury and arrived at a beautiful estate owned by Lord Coventry. We didn't stay there long. We had our dinner and pushed on. We arrived at another spot, settled down for two hours, were called to move again, got about two hours sleep and moved again. We finally arrived at a spot just outside Banbury.

We were warned to move early this morning. We got ready and waited. Nothing happened. Finally at about 8:00 p.m. the word came through that the move had been cancelled until the next day.

We had a good run today. I waited behind the convoy to pick up some bikes that had broken down. By the time I was ready to push off, the convoy had gotten well out of sight. As a matter of fact, I never did catch up with them again! I passed through Towcester, Harwell and finally stopped at Rise- ley. I was supposed to meet the rest there but found out on arriving that the scheme had been cancelled. We hung around the place long enough for Paul to get some tea and then headed back. I passed through Guildford, Dorking, Reigate, Tunbridge-Wells and eventually arrived back home. I found I was the first one back. I learned later in the day that the lads would be held out for another 48 hours so I really got the jump on them.

It was wonderful sleeping in a bed again. Bill Elder, (who had been left beind in charge) and I went for breakfast at 8:30 a.m. As there were no troops around I didn't have any parades. I just spent the day thinking about home and getting some letters off.

Now It's My Turn in the Hospital

April 23, 1943.

I didn't mention that I was going into the hospital. I didn't want anyone to worry. I checked in on Monday, visited some of our own lads with mail that had arrived for them then checked myself into the officers' ward where I was assigned bed #25. The ward has 30 beds but there are only 15 officers at the present time. I sat around most of the day and did my best to get acquainted with the "inmates." After dinner the doctor came in to see me and said that he would work on me in the morning.

The next day I was up early, washed and shaved. When I got back to bed it had a 'No Breakfast' sign on it. I carried on until eleven when they took me to the operating room. I got a spinal (think it's tops) and never felt a thing. The hernia had developed a lot and started to give me a wee bit of trouble so I thought I'd better have it out. I had a good cup of tea when I returned to my bed and when supper arrived I was in there like a duck! It took about eight hours for the feeling to come back into my legs and lower body.

I had a good night's sleep and woke up to breakfast of bacon, eggs and toast. Not bad for a well man! The doctor was in to see me and he thinks that I'm doing just fine. He tells me that I will be in bed about 14 days and then one month convalescence ... that shouldn't be too hard to take.

Today is Good Friday and there are services throughout the hospital. It was very cold and they had to put the stoves on in the ward. I feel pretty good today and can't see why they will keep me so long in bed. I feel as if I could get up right now. I had visits this evening from six of the lads. I was most pleased to see them. They sure are a great bunch of boys.

May 1, 1943.

Easter Monday came and went with me still in bed. Writing from bed is most difficult and it will be a real treat when I can sit down on a chair and write from a table. Now that I'm feeling much better, bed is becoming a real bore and even though I'm resting my posterior on an inflated rubber tire, still the old bed becomes kind of hard. I've had wonderful attention ... wouldn't want the bill scored against my account. I have spent most of the last eleven days eating, washing and reading ... not bad fare.

On Tuesday I had my stitches out – eleven in all. The doctor said everything was in perfect shape. All of my lads who are in hospital paid me a visit. They think its funny to see me in bed.

I was permitted to sit up on Friday with my feet hanging down by the side of the bed. Of course, they watched me closely so I wouldn't put my feet on the floor. The war news that Tunis and Berzerta had fallen caused much excitement in the ward. Look's like things will now move in earnest. If we could hit them hard by summer we would all be home by Christmas.

May 15, 1943.

I got away from the hospital on Monday at eight and took the staff car to the train. I got to London where I changed trains for Hereford. Eventually I arrived at the Massey Convalescent Home. I was met at the door by the butler, who in his fine English accent said, "I will show you to your room, Sir." Next I was introduced to the housekeeper and senior hostess, both very nice. I met the doctor who took me to my quarters. There were about twenty officers sitting around playing cards and reading.

The next day I was called by the butler at eight. He brought me my shoes and clothes. This kind of service is going to kill me! After breakfast I took a walk through the mansion. Each room was well carpeted and every wall has paintings of lords and ladies of the manor. There is a grand playroom overlooking the terrace where we can do arts and crafts, run electric trains, play the latest records; have a go at a set of drums, mend toys for refugee children. The library was the next stop. It's the latest thing in personal comfort. There's another room with a fine billiard table. When I want to recall my misspent youth I go there for a few games ... usually for a couple of hours.

On Wednesday I took a real good walk through the estate. There is a garden that has every fruit, flower or vegetable in existence. The estate covers 5000 acres. After supper I took a long walk over the fields crowded with sheep and cattle. I came to a quaint old church where I spent time reading epitaphs to the honoured dead of the 16th and 17th century. It would be great to be convalescing in Canada but no such luck. The padres are here until the business is over.

May 24, 1943.

I spent the weekend in Oxford visiting my aunt and uncle and their family. I hitchhiked into Hereford and got the train to Oxford. The Rowlands were all home and Roy their son whom I hadn't seen, was on a fourteen day leave. He's rather a pleasant young lad who has been in the army since August '39.

Roy and I spent Saturday morning walking along the Thames. The morning was beautiful as women and children were bathing here and there along its banks. A small sailing boat caught my eye where a soldier, probably home on leave, was making up for lost time. As usual I never miss a thing!

I left Oxford on Sunday noon by train. The countryside was lovely. All the common vegetables are above ground and in some cases early potatoes are being dug. It is quite the grandest piece of English country that I have seen. I hitched in from the station and arrived in time for tea. It looks like I'll be here until June 10th since I have to speak at the Welsh General Assembly on the 9th. I do miss the Unit and will be pleased to get back. I have been seven weeks away from the Regiment. Just a wee bit too long. Me thinks I will have to start all over again.

May 31, 1943.

I had an interesting experience in Hereford the other day. I had gone in for a meal with another officer and on the bus coming out we sat in front of a gypsy who unsolicited, began to tell my fortune: "Your grey hair indicates the commencement of a multitude of worries. You have a wife who is breaking her heart to see you. In about three months you will see her but you will have to go across water to do so." Since I was in civilian clothes that wasn't a bad bit of prophecy. I only hope she was right. I would have given her a sixpence but when she told the other officer that he was going to become a father (he hadn't seen his wife in two years) the truth of her deliberations became highly suspect!

I have spent much of the week sight-seeing through Wales. We have visited Brecon and Abergavenny. The Welsh people seem more free and easy going than the English. Their brogue comes next to the Dubliners!

June 10, 1943.

On Tuesday I headed for Menai Bridge, a long train ride with many changes in between. I was met by the men from the Assembly at journey's end. I was received by the Welsh Assembly as Canada's delegation, at 10:00 a.m. on Wednesday. I gave my address and I must say was warmly received. After-wards I was presented with a book of sermons by Lord Clwyd, an ex-moderator of their church. He was a grand old man and gave me a real handshake. I must say that there was little of the Assembly's business that I understood since it was all in the Welsh language. I managed to laugh when the rest laughed so I guess I made out all right.

I got away from Bangor at noon today and didn't arrive home until nine. It was a long journey and I was glad when it ended. The padre who had taken my place had gone so I got my own bed back. I had a lot of mail waiting for me and that was certainly uplifting. The news of the fall of Pantelleuse is good news ... we are moving forward and homeward.

It's Great to Be Back on the Job

June 18, 1943.

I've spent most of my time just getting reacquainted with the Unit. There have been many changes and I saw a lot of new men in our midst. We have a new second-in-command and the C.O. is on a month's course so I haven't seen him. Getting back on the job has been quite an experience but I suppose preaching is like riding a bike – one never forgets how. I had two good parades and was glad to see so many old faces again. With my hospital visitations and my educational work, it won't take me long to get back into full gear.

I was busy conducting 'Padre's Hour' today. I dealt with a couple of domestic problems that were so vile they made me extremely angry. One included a lad's wife who is sleeping around back in Canada and leaves the children alone at night to go out and have her fun. We are just away long enough for things to go wrong. I expect that I will have some wives writing to me regarding their husbands but so far nothing has come along. I hope it never does. On the whole the men are behaving pretty well. One or two of the single lads have got themselves into jams and have had to marry. Of course a Canadian is a good catch here (their pay is one of the big considerations).

June 29, 1943.

It looks like many problems have awaited my return. I can't remember when I had so many men come to see me about the same problem. By the time I got through reading evidence on unfaithful wives in Canada, I was ready to have a warm bath to clean myself off. I must have written ten letters home. I wonder what some of the wives will think when they hear from me. I bet they call me one big busybody. Since I'm far away I fancy it will do me no harm.

I had a couple of lads in to see me about getting married. Gradually our lads are falling for the English girls. I asked one of them how he came to meet his girl and he told me that he was out horseback riding and found her in a ditch (apparently she had fallen off her horse). I thought it was a good story.

On Sunday the Padre was very busy. I had three parades and got through without any aches or pains. The boys thought I gave them a blast (perhaps I did). I was going after them on unfaithfulness and I let a few strong phrases slip into my vocabulary.

This morning was taken up with discussion groups. We discusssed our place in a postwar society. The boys have a lot to say about it but some of them think that things will be just as hard for the soldier after this war as it was after the last. Others, in the majority I might add, feel if we lay plans now, things will turn out all right and we will all go back to a better Canada. By the time I finish I fancy I will pretty well know what the Canadian soldier wants.

July 8, 1943.

I wonder how many more months we will have to put in. Time is moving right along. I am now well settled and comfortable in a new home. This time it is with 'C' company and not with H.Q. It's a perfect set up and I now have the company of Bill Elder and Harvey Adams. I have a whole room to myself and one lovely springbed with a view from my window that would knock your eye out. Castles are becoming old hat ... suppose I'll have to have one when I get back to Canada.

I spent Saturday morning looking up the local clergy to see if I could use their churches. I will be taking the civilian congregation along with the troops. I'm sure the men will appreciate such a change so long as there is a good-looking choir of ladies to add local colour.

It is getting difficult to relate much of the news. Security prevents a lot of the telling. The war continues slowly but progressively. I have no idea how long it will be before we get into action. I was reading the other day of the critical illness of Goering and Hitler. I wish that Providence would step in and remove them from the earth. They have caused so much grief we can well be rid of them.

This morning I had an interview with Lady Downe, who owns the estate and house where we are located. She has given me instructions to use all the vegetables we need from her garden as well as the fruit from the many trees. After my talk with her I visited a Lord Hancock, who is running a garden party this afternoon. He wanted the use of our band and a couple of boxers, all of which I was able to arrange. He is a personal friend of the King's and has promised that if he comes up this way he will see I have a chance to meet him. Looks like I'm going real 'nobby'.

July 12, 1943.

One of my jobs is to look after the needs of the 24th Field Ambulance. I had about seventy men in a discussion group during my 'Padre's Hour'. I also interviewed a French laddie who told me that his wife was going to have a baby and was worried about it. He had the idea that he should be home with her for the occasion. He gave me some of her letters to read. The French sure have a way with words. Ah me, but I smiled!

I held my church service in an old church that dated back to the 1100's. The boys were most impressed with all they saw and I was a bit startled to find myself preaching from a pulpit that was used by some of the outstanding men in the Church of England. I was wondering how the folk would relish a reformer in their pulpit. Of course, they didn't seem to know so everything went along just fine. One man said to me, "The thing I liked about your service was that it was short."

Today I took the company on a tour of the King's estate Sandringham. It was a wonderful experience for us all. We were taken through the grounds by a police escort and were shown where the late King died and the place where he used to broadcast. We were taken to the church on the estate where the Royal Family worships. I met the King's chaplain – a young Irish lad from Dublin (that put us on the ground floor). He gave us a grand tour and lecture.

Originally I got there through Lady Downe who had the agent of the estate for tea last week. I never miss an opportunity, that's me. I plan to take the whole Regiment through it.

We were all excited when we heard the news that the Canadians had landed in Sicily. Our Unit is still here in England and since we are at the tail end of things, we probably will be the last to get in.

July 18, 1943.

I've just returned from another scheme. I had a wash, shave and feel much better. I couldn't help but think as I lay trying to keep the rain out of my eyes, what a fellow will do when he has to.

The news from Sicily shows things are going well. The Canadians are more than doing their job. I fancy that will be the direction we will go when our time comes; however, it may be some time before we get into the action. If the breaks are with us and the going looks good, we may throw everything at them to bring the whole business to a quick end. When our time comes we will be ready.

While I'm living out in the country I come in twice a week in the evenings for interviews. I have just concluded four ... two wanting to get rid of their wives; two wanting to get married.

I had two parades this morning and we took the pipe band along. I never saw so many people hanging out of the windows as I did in the village. One old lad told me that it was the first time his wife had been up to make his breakfast in all their married life! I had a great experience after the service. I was asked to take the salute for the home guard. This I did with much pride especially when I learned that some Lord so-and-so was the company commander and would have to give me the salute. I tell you I felt like Montgomery! When I came back and told the officers the story they had a fit. It just seems that you can't keep this wee man down.

J3July 24, 1943

I've spent most of my time visiting the hospitals and holding interviews for the lads. We have our men spread all over the place and it's hard to locate them all. I think the lads realize that if they are ill there is a chance of them not getting back to the Unit. We must be up to strength at all times; if one leaves another is there to take his place. Fortunately we don't have too many sick which is a good thing. The lads are getting a lot of home problems these days. The sooner the war is over the sooner will end some of the domestic strife. Everything looks rather bad from a distance.

I had a long chat with the C.O. Apparently he does not know when or where our next move will be. We are supposed to be here for about six weeks and then ... well we just don't know. Possibly we will go back to the south or then again they may shove us off with the rest to Sicily. It certainly looks like Sicily will soon be in our hands.

It didn't take the Vatican long to raise its voice against the bombing of Rome. Seems to have taken some time to realize what bombing can do. There are just as many sacred churches in this country. The people here are certainly not taking too kindly to the criticism. It seems to me that human life is the most valuable commodity – certainly more valuable than historical buildings.

The boys left this morning on a week's scheme. I was left behind with some of the boxers so I gathered them up for a party being put on this afternoon by some of the locals. They put on a real show and are, as always, received very well for their efforts. After dinner they played bridge (they go for it in a big way here). There was a prize of ten shillings and the good Canadian Padre won it. I never remember getting better hands. They seem to have some idea that I'm a shark!

July 26, 1943.

Yesterday evening I preached in the Church of England. I enjoyed the service although the people don't come out to church in droves in this country. Since I have done nothing else but preach for the Anglicans over here, I will have to learn Presbyterianism all over again. After the service I went home with the minister for dinner. The first thing he asked me was what I would like to drink. I think he was surprised when I asked for a soft one.

There seems to be a lot of airforce activity going on. They must be coming in from a big raid. They certainly are turning on the heat these days. The Canadians are doing their fair share in Sicily. Our lads are very anxious to get into it. Maybe they will before too long. I only hope that we can get into the business soon to help finish it off quickly.

July 28, 1943.

We have had a very interesting scheme these past two days. We moved off on Monday night and it was quite the business getting around in the jeep in the dark. We got bedded down in the wee hours and since it was a warm night it was a treat to sleep out. After dinner we were on the move again. We passed through some grand country but as evening wore on we were plugging through some pretty rough bush. At midnight we were to make an attack on the "enemy" so about eleven we crawled into position. Zero hour came and in we went to the 'attack' which brought us to a large river over which we had to cross. Was I ever wet! I stopped on the other side to empty my boots. I think I got more than my share. I moved along in the darkness with the men, feeling quite proud that I had done so well in the crossing. All of a sudden "bingo' down I went into another river-hole! This time I didn't bother to make any changes but marched on the next three miles feeling like a sheet in a washing machine. At about three we drove the "enemy" back and captured their positions. At this point we parked in a wheat field. Elder and Doc Boyden came up to me as I was removing my boots and socks. Without a word they just lay down on the ground and went to sleep. They were cold so I gathered some sheaves to cover them up. Once in a while Bill would say "So I left Belleville for this!" "Ah yes", I said, "but think of the fun we're having."

August 4, 1943.

I had many highly-coloured interviews to contend with. This war must end soon or else we will have to get all the men out of Canada if we are going to save Canada's home life! There's a lot of monkey business going on. The thing I'm finding more and more is that it is not the most recent marriages where most of the trouble is developing but marriages that have taken place anywhere from seven to ten years ago. Could people live together that long without any real long term commitment? I'm afraid I haven't the answer.

On Saturday evening I put on the Regimental films for a war charity affair. The place was packed and we added about 50 pounds to the effort. It was rather interesting to see the lords, ladies and commoners mixing together. They sure have a lot to learn in this country. Had I to live here in this society I think I would be a bit of a rebel.

I had one large Regimental parade on Sunday. We had about 400 present. I did something I have never done before. I singled out the officers and gave them a blast. Bill Elder was telling me afterwards that some of them said it made them feel rather cheap and ashamed. I struck home when I talked about officers learning to discipline themselves before being ready to do something with their men. They can't expect to drink all night and then come to the orderly rooms and charge the men with drunkenness. Apparently some of the officers headed for cover after the service.

Tomorrow I will be three years in the army. My, it seems like a long time. Daily the light of victory and peace is enlarging and somehow I feel it can't be too long before we reach the end of the way. The news has just come in that Catania has fallen. The Russians too have captured Orel which means the Germans are being pushed back all the time. Soon Hitler like Mussie will be looking for a place to hide.

I'm afraid what I was doing today I can't put down on paper. Someday I will have a lot of stories to tell.

August 8, 1943.

Today I met the King, Queen and Princesses. It all happened like this: The Royal Family was inspecting a guard of honour and as usual as the official photographer, I was on hand. Unfortunately the morning was dark and very dull with the odd shower thrown in for good measure. The Royal Party arrived looking stunning. The King was met by the officer of the guard and the usual welcome was extended. Next the Royal Party proceeded to inspect the troops. First went the King followed by the Queen and the Princesses. It was a grand sight. Unfortunately the sun refused to shine; however, I followed them with my camera and while I know that the shots will be poor, still I will have them. They soon came to the end of their inspection. The King spotted my collar and camera and walked right over to me. He asked my name and shook my hand. In the meantime Paul grabbed my camera and started shooting pictures of the greeting. The King asked me how long I had been in the service, where my church was in Toronto, how I liked my job and the kind of responses I got from the men. He then said that he was very pleased that I was preaching to his people that night. I told him that it was my honour. The Queen came forward and the King moved off. She gave me that million dollar smile of hers and shook my hand. "You have a wonderful lot of troops", she said. I replied, "I'm very proud of them". "I'm sure you are", she said. She too asked me how long I had been with them. When I told her she commented that it is not often a chaplain can stay with one unit for that length of time. She also reminded me of the evening service and hoped that it would be dry as it was an open air affair.

The Princesses were standing by during all of this taking everything in. I think they must get tired of all the formality. After the proceedings were over we had a group picture taken with all the officers sitting with their Majesties for the occasion. From there we walked with them to church. I had the honour of walking with the King's secretary and agent and in front of us was the Queen with the children. I found that I was given the very front seat, a distance of about ten feet from the Royal Family.

The service was very simple and plain and as I watched the Royal pew I noticed the Royal Family entering right into the service. Margaret Rose, however, didn't seem so interested in the service as she was looking around to see who was there. Now and then the Princesses smiled my way. I thought that they were just like any other children. I fancy they saw a few things that brought a smile to their lips.

After the service the Royal Family retired and then the congregation left. I went for dinner to the chaplain's rectory and rehashed the doings of the day. T'was a great morning and one that will live long in the memory of all whose good fortune it was to be in attendance. I felt that I more than shared in the honours. In the evening I arrived at the Royal Gardens with the King's chaplain. It was raining like Hades. There was a good number of people present including all the King's staff. I did my best and gave it all I had. After the service the King's recorder came and asked me for some part of the service that he had missed. Apparently I went too fast for his shorthand. I understand that a record of all that went on is presented. Afterwards I was taken for dinner to York cottage where all the Royal Family were born. We had a duck dinner. Not hard to take. When I came home around midnight, I was indeed ready for bed. The day and the opportunities were beyond my imagination and I never dreamed it would be my good fortune to meet the King and Queen, worship with them and preach on their estate. It was a great day for the Irish!

August 31, 1943.

We've arrived at the end of another month. Soon we will be a year away from home. It's far too long and I hope that the next few months will bring us a lot of changes. I have again been busy with interviews especially ones for marriage. I'm thinking that our lads have gone "dotty" over the lassies here. I only hope that everything will turn out happy for them. One of the lads told me that he was staying in England after the war. When I asked him why, he told me that the girl's mother would never allow her daughter to go so far away. When I reminded him that his mother let him come, he said he would use that approach from now on. Ah me, but it's some business!

After our Divisional parade on Sunday, Elder and I went out to visit a family I had met in March on a scheme. Coming home we picked up a South of Ireland civilian. He had a few drinks and I never listened to so much 'malarky'. He sang a few Irish songs to keep us amused. T'was good I was driving for folks would have thought we were on a real tear! The fellow had been living in England for eighteen years and you'd swear he just got off the boat. In our excitement we missed the road and only by good luck did we find another that took us back to our camp.

September 4, 1943.

I've organized a new Regimental sports program that was well received by the C.O. when I submitted it for his approval. There are a few new officers interested so I'm putting them to work. My noon broadcasts are still very popular and are going full steam ahead. I still have trouble with the Russian names but since they are doing so well all I need to say to get over my part is, "The Russians are still moving on". Always a diplomat, that's me.

I've just concluded several interviews, a few letters to Canada on domestic problems and one 'Padre's Hour'. I still have them coming in for permission to marry. I turned down a couple of lads today ... I didn't think they knew their ladies long enough. To them I'm a bit of a mug but I sometimes get a little fed up with some of the unreasonable demands that are made.

I put in the morning preparing for the Sabbath. As I was writing my sermon I was wishing I was going to be preaching in a Canadian pulpit. I'm going to be an excited man once again when I stand with a Canadian congregation before me.

September 10, 1943.

I held my church parade outside and had 400 out. I just got finished when down came the rain. I was thinking the lads might wish it would happen before the service! Bill Armstrong, Tony Allan and Bill Leonard returned to our Unit. Payne, Mitchell and Crozier have gone to take their place in the holding unit.

I got word today that one of our lads died in hospital. This is our first casualty since coming over. I wrote his parents in Toronto. It will certainly be a hard blow for them. He was just 23.

The news of Italy's surrender came at 6:00 p.m. on Wednesday and the men went wild. It will make a big difference and it is sure to shorten the war by a few months. It will be interesting to see what the reaction will be in the conquered countries.

I was off on a scheme today. Along the roads people were out giving us apples and tea. I don't know where they get it all. We went through some country and cities that I hadn't seen before so it was a new experience. I had the opportunity of seeing Portsmouth and Gosport and here we saw what destruction had been caused by the Germans. When you see it, you can't seem to work up much sympathy for the pounding they are now getting.

September 17, 1943.

I was in to see Southhampton on Sunday. I thought we had seen everything along the lines of destruction a few days ago but here we saw a city flattened! I'm sure the loss of life has been tremendous. I've been kept busy with interviews most mornings. One lad was in to see if he could marry by proxy. When I replied that it would be impossible he told me that we have voted by proxy and he really didn't see any difference. What's a Padre to do? I know he left feeling that I was no help. I seem to be still writing letters home for men in trouble. I do wish some of the wives in Canada would smarten up. I'd like to meet some of them face to face.

The Royal Guard pictures arrived for the men and belive it or not it took me all morning getting them out. We have had a few mix-ups but with thirty pounds worth to sort out, no wonder. We are still dealing with the postwar world in my 'Padre's Hour' and to be sure the lads have a lot to say about it. I hope they get half of what they want.

Bill Elder and Dusty Miller got their captaincies so I had a ginger ale on their promotions. They didn't seem to be too excited about it but it's great that they have gone up. We got some records from the wives and mothers of the lads and I played them today. It's a real lift for the boys to hear the voices of their loved ones.

September 29, 1943.

I had a few personal interviews this morning. Some of the men are still having wife trouble. I am becoming a real past master in domestic problems and how they should be solved. I bet some of the wives would like to get their hands on me; however, not quite as much as I would like to arrange for a personal interview with some of them!

One of the padres was telling me that there would not be any churches left when we got back to Canada. I told him that since I was Irish I could get a job in Eatons. He asked if I would speak for him as well. We had quite a laugh and why not.

Tomorrow I'm leaving with the advance party for a new location. They haven't kept us long where we are now located. If changing around tends to keep us all happy and content then we are getting our share of it.

We arrived at our new location and found it most pleasing. If they are planning to keep us here for the winter then it will be a good show. I have a very nice billet with a lovely garden in the back and a million dollar view.

Duncan, Fisher and I went into town this morning for breakfast. Believe it or not we had eggs, bacon, chips and lots of coffee. We attended the Presbyterian church in the afternoon and received a number of invitations for supper ... we start with the minister on Wednesday. It looks like we will be well-looked after.

I got lost in the blackout on the way home. I'll be glad when I can see the lights at night again. I had an idea that since things were going so well over here that they might let up on the blackouts. So far they are continuing as usual. I think one of the things I will do when I return home is just put on every light in the house and go outside and watch them burn.

Destination Unknown

By the time this letter arrives home I will be at an unknown destination. Where we are going is anyone's guess. The only thing we know is that we are on a ship that serves meals I haven't seen since we left Canada. It is going to be an awful letdown when we go back to army rations. We are all wondering were the next stop will be. It is difficult to write without censorship since so much depends upon secrecy. So little goes on while sailing it's a bit difficult to gather up much news. I am now a week at sea and getting used to it. We had a very rough sea yesterday and I think it affected all. I never saw so many sea-sick. It was most obvious at mealtime. So far I have managed to make every meal and have missed being sick. I don't know whether I'm a good sailor or just lucky. It's still a mystery where we are headed. I feel we are going to end up somewhere in Africa. Just a year ago I was on my way to England. I didn't expect we could get a whole year in. Anyway it gave me a chance to get around to see a few places. I was rather lucky to get my last leave to Ireland. I'm wondering how long it will be before mail starts arriving from home. I'm worried how long it will take our mail to reach its destination. ...

I don't know what the weather is like in Canada but we are now basking in glorious sunshine! This is our eleventh day at sea. On Sunday we had a wonderful day. I conducted five services all of which were very well attended. I think one of the highlights of the trip has been the absence of alcohol. It's a treat to travel on sobriety. The food continues to be tops and I am now wondering how I will ever get used to army food again. The sailing has been just perfect and the lads have, for the most part, got their sea legs. ...

We are now fourteen days aboard ship. It has been a long time but somehow it has gone by quickly. I feel that we are near journey's end. Yesterday was our big moment. We got our first glimpse of land. It was a strange sight especially since we hadn't seen any for thirteen days. Through my glasses I could see some gracious sights which brought back vividly some of the strange and weird tales I have heard. It will be a grand day when I can tell the whole story. Believe it or not I am suffering from a severe sunburn which I got while lying out on deck yesterday. If this is going to be the first taste of our winter then I'm all for it. We got a daily news bulletin and things, while a bit slow, seem to be moving well in our favour. I would imagine that the German would soon see the futility of his effort. Perhaps Canadian newspapers have something out that might clear up the mystery of our whereabouts. ...

I am now on solid land after spending nineteen days at sea. The trip was an interesting one and somehow I didn't mind the time at all, however, when I put my feet on Italian soil I thanked God for the safe voyage.

The Business Now Begins

November 13, 1943.

We are now strictly censored and it will be difficult to give out very much information. On arriving we were greeted by the Italian civilians. As we passed through the cities we saw first-hand what war could do to a nation. All along the roads could be seen refugees on all kinds of wagons, carting their goods. They were going both ways so it was hard to decide what was going on. The poverty was sickening. Men, women and children were walking in rags and bare feet and looked as though they hadn't had a bath for ages. Filth and more filth was evident everywhere you turned. The sidewalks were used as toilets by all without regard. The little children in rags with dirty faces, scabby hands and feet made me very sad. All in all it is very hard to explain. One has to see it to believe it.

We came to our area and I couldn't help but be thankful that our families were so far away from such desolation. We are quartered in a vineyard but it hasn't all the colour that one associates with such places. It smells terribly and we are living in the open. The nights are very cold but the days would burn you up. Just a few minutes ago I had an open air bath. I needed it, but the trouble is that you have no privacy. They don't seem to mind such things here and I'd rather be clean than worry about the civilians watching me. We are pretty well settled and so far our food is good. After the meals aboard ship it's a bit hard getting back.

Already some of the lads have been off sight-seeing and oh, the sights they have seen! I had a chat with the "Telegram" reporter and he assured me that he'd be getting the news home soon.

November 14, 1943.

This is my second letter from this new land. Right now I am settled in a tent with a strong wind blowing. I was up very early this morning. It was a bit uncomfortable shaving in cold water but I managed through all right. All of us are a pretty queer sight as we tumble from our pup tents the first thing in the morning. We have managed to get a tent up where we eat and call it our mess. It is much better than eating out in the open especially since there are a flock of flies ready to follow the food right into your mouth! At 9:30 a.m. I held my first church parade. Brigadier Kitching was on hand and read the lesson. He has been in action with the First Division and that gives him a real '*leg-on*' with the boys. After dinner I took 'B' company on a '*Cook's Tour*' and we sure saw a few '*Wonders of the World!*' It was very dark when we arrived home. I ate supper and sacked out about 6:00 p.m. During the night a storm blew up and off went my tent leaving me sitting in the rain. Stew Bell was right next to me and I think he thought we were hit with something. During the night I kicked off my battledress onto the ground and when I came to get into it this morning it was as wet as the deuce.

November 15, 1943.

I think from the little we have gone through so far, all of us will be very easily satisfied when we do get home. I'm doing the best I can to dry myself out and since the sun is coming up I feel sure we will make the grade. It's early morning still and I have very little laid on for the day. I had hoped to take a couple of the companies out on a tour but lost my transport for another job. We'll try again tomorrow. As far as I can see, the people here will be destitute for years. Their homes, property and families are broken. As I drive through their streets, I often wonder how they ever allowed themselves to be so unwisely led. They sure could use a real bath but I suppose that's the least of their worries. All day many of them hang around the camp selling wine, fruit or simply begging for hand-outs. The fruit looks very good although we have orders to wash and peel it before we attempt to eat it. It looks like I'll be saving lots of money here. There is really nothing to spend it on. I should have a good holiday bank saved when I get back.

November 21, 1943.

I have been on the go this past week and already have seen quite a bit of Italy. It certainly is not the sunny spot that some would make it out to be. I have seen more mud and have lived in so much of it that I now feel like a bit of a rat. I think it has rained for about eight days. I really don't think it knows when to quit. I thought Ireland was bad for the rain, or for that matter England, but neither of them are any match for this country.

There are many very good highways quite like our own. I went over some and at times I thought I was drifting along the Princess Elizabeth. The people use their cattle for ploughing, drawing water and pulling carts. There are hundreds of donkeys here and they are used for drawing heavier loads. The country is so mountainous that it makes it difficult for the poor animals to get along.

On Sunday I had a big church parade. A few Italians who stood around wondered what it was all about. I met an Italian who speaks English very well and he has helped me out on a number of occasions. I go shopping with him and today he took me where I can get a decent bath. I have managed to pick up a few words but not enough to get very far. Should we stay here for a while I think I will be able to collect enough words to make myself understood.

It's been a week since I last saw a newspaper. The war could be all over and we wouldn't know a thing about it. From all accounts everyone seems to think it will end in the spring and that would be very good news. We heard the other day that Churchill said it would be over in 1944. All I pray is that his prediction is accurate.

I seem to be able to make a shirt last me all week. I manage to wash in my mess tin and so far I have failed to become lousy but I don't know how long that will last!

November 23, 1943.

I am now in a new place and it is a bit of heaven when compared to what we had. We have a roof over our heads and that is something in a country where it seems to do nothing else but rain and rain. It is now about eleven days since we saw the sun. They make no mistake when they call this the Italian rainy season. You can understand how slowly the war moves under such conditions. I haven't actually seen any fighting although I have seen some of the results. I'm having a lot of fun with the money. They use the lire and one lire equals a penny. Since they use neither gold nor silver, all you get is a handful of paper money. If you make a transaction of say five shillings, and you get change, you would think you conducted the biggest business deal of your entire life!

The town we are now in is not so bad. It's about the best I've seen to date. The homes are "box-shaped" and are pushed together without apparent shape or design. I visited a private home today and was surprised to see how immaculate it was. I have a little Italian soldier who takes me around. He lived in New York for a number of years and speaks perfect English. I'm gradually picking up a few words and should do much better as time goes by. I have arranged with him to start some classes and tonight we are going to have our first one. It doesn't appear to be too difficult a language as most of the words are pronounced as they are spelled. Our lads are managing to get along very well and so far Paul has found a place to get my washing and pressing done. I get a laugh out of the way he tries to speak to the locals. He does it all with his hands and so help me the people have no problem understanding him. Yesterday we got our car. It's not a jeep (thank goodness). They call it an 800 cwt. It's going to be very comfortable. I can sleep and eat in it when I'm out in the field. It will add a lot of colour to my colourless life!

On Sunday I had a very large church parade. We held it in a courtyard. I was told that Mussolini used it when he came to give a speech to the students. I'm sure had he been listening he would have wondered what was happening to his "created paradise". The feeling among the people towards him is very severe (of course you can't always depend upon what you hear). I have a suspicion that some of them just know how to play their cards. I'm going to be very cautious. To date I have seen a lot of the country. Geographically it offers very many looks: you can go for miles along plains and then suddenly you strike very mountainous regions. It does make it very difficult to manoeuvre by car. I would say that the soldiers in action so far have done a wonderful job achieving so much under such hard circumstances.

November 24, 1943.

I received letters today from several wives concerning their relationships with their husbands. One said frankly she didn't want to see her husband anymore as she had found someone whom she now loved; the other was willing to wait until the war was over before she made up her mind – a safe attitude from a financial point of view. I will be ever so pleased when this war ends, for then the constant domestic grumblings which I continue to have to deal with, will be over. While my work has a lot of positive sides, still there is much rotten stuff that confronts me. Somehow I will be relieved when the last shot is fired but even then some of the men will be going home to more conflict.

We are gradually getting settled into our new location and so far we haven't too much to kick about. Our food is very good and our living quarters beat sleeping outdoors. I bought myself a washing-stand outfit ... it looks like a travelling circus! It has a mirror, towel rack, soap pan and good-sized washing dish. I paid about $3.00 our money for it.

From the news we received today, it appears that the Germans have done a lot of damage as they retreated here. I think when they realize that they can't win, they will also have to contend with a number of civilians who have many scores to settle.

November 27, 1943.

Yesterday we had a good day and I managed to arrange a soccer game with an English unit. We had the time of our lives and a real game thrown in. Despite their obvious knowledge of the game they managed to only beat us by a goal. In fact, they scored the winning goal in the last few minutes of play. I refereed the game so you can see that everything was on the up and up! I have seen some excellent playing fields here. They tell me that the Italians are real masters of the game. We'll have to give them a go at our earliest convenience. This afternoon I visited the local Protestant minister. It was an interesting experience. I brought along our '*English to Italian*' book and it was wonderful how well we made out. At the end of our conversation his wife made us some lemon tea – it was a real treat and went down very well. I'm holding a service for the lads tomorrow night in his church and already the lads are expressing that they are anxious to be there. The church will only hold about a hundred so I'm hoping that we don't get an overflow crowd. We learned from the minister that there are about 80,000 Protestants in Italy, with Florence being their main headquarters. The work is naturally carried by our home missions and the States apparently is their best supporter.

Tomorrow I'm taking the Unit on a sight-seeing trip, one that is considered tops here – Pompeii. As I walked through the ruins in preparation for the tour, my mind drifted back to my early days at school. I'm sure the lads will thoroughly enjoy it.

November 29, 1943.

I conducted five services yesterday. When night came I was a bit tired. I also took about 400 of the lads on a sight-seeing tour. We visited one of Mussolini's modern cities and we were all taken with it. It compared in modern architecture to what one might see along Bay St. It was extremely clean and that in itself says a lot for over here. I saw men and women well dressed going about their business. What a change from what we have been used to!

Last night I conducted a service in the Protestant church in the town and it was so unique in every way. I know that I will never forget it. About 50 of the lads came along and that was enough to fill the place since there were some of the local members present. Through an interpreter, we were welcomed by the local minister and then I started in. Since we have all denominations in the Unit I thought I would give everybody a share in the service. I got an Anglican to read the Old Testament, a Baptist to read the New, a United Church and Presbyterian to take up the offering. All in all it was a most inspiring service and left an impression on all. I conducted a communion service too and the minister told me that to his knowledge that was the first one ever conducted in English in a Protestant church in Italy. Gord Keyes was the 'liner-upper' for the whole do and did a splendid job. We sang for our closing hymn "Abide With Me" and when we finished the Italian congregation sang it in their "lingo" for us. I must say I never did hear people sing like that. They had wonderful voices. The boys want another one next Sunday so I'll certainly oblige. From the interpreter I learned that they have a very hard time with their faith. I feel that we left them feeling very good and I trust helped to inspire confidence in their work.

We had a lovely day yesterday and this morning there is no sign of rain. Maybe we will get a few days free from showers. While we haven't heard any war news for days, we got a rumour last night that things were moving fast for us. I pray that the end is near.

December 1, 1943.

No matter where one goes there is talk about an early victory. I don't know if it is because we are so close to the Germans that such a spirit is so prevalent but one gets it not only from the troops but also from the Italians. It is a great feeling and one that I am more than willing to adopt.

We have been told that there will be days even weeks, when we won't be able to get mail out. Yesterday I was busy in the hospitals. We have one close by and I have eight men there, all in with a touch of the flu. The change of climate affects some of them and the food plays tricks with their stomachs. In the afternoon I went 40 miles to see another bunch of the lads. Paul and I got lost in the mountains for about an hour (my map reading slipped up a bit). After driving through goats, sheep and a few refugees, we finally found the right road. I had a good visit with all the lads and while there met a lot of doctors and nurses I hadn't seen since we left Canada. They have a wonderful set up.

Last night I had interviews in my office. I had about five men in to see me. Two were men who showed me letters from unfaithful wives and as a result were to see me to have their allowances cut-off. For the sake of our homes in Canada I will be glad when the end comes. Many of our domestic difficulties wouldn't occur if the men were home.

The adjutant has come in to say that Colonel Ralston is paying us a visit this morning. I trust he will have some goods news for us. Maybe he will tell us how long we have to wait before we jump ship for home!

December 2, 1943.

After dinner today I had a wonderful bath in the local hospital. We pay about 20¢ and believe me it is worth it. I manage to get one about every third day so you see I'm doing my best to keep the lice away.

I have had quite a demand from the lads for another service in the local Protestant church. I'm conducting one Sunday night. This morning I went alone to see the minister, Dr. Pedro Nesterini, and managed to make fairly good conversation with him. He and his people are all pleased that we came and he tells me it has done much in their town to help cement relationships.

This afternoon I visited a town about ten miles away and from what I saw, it was by far the cleanest and most attractive I have come across. I went to look over a sports field and it turned out to be a regular show place. They have one of the best soccer fields I have ever seen and a track which compares well with anything that we have at home. Basketball and tennis courts were all well arranged and some of the local civilians were having the time of their lives. For a moment, as I stood on top of the stands, I thought I was in Varsity Stadium. I will now get busy and arrange a sports day for the Unit. The troops are all C.B. in this area and I can tell you that it doesn't go down very well with Canadians who have been used to a lot of freedom. The more I can get them out in an organized way, the less trouble we will have. Me thinks the Padre's job out here is going to be a real tester and I hope I measure up. Our C.O. who has just returned from the front on a visit, tells me the padres are doing an outstanding job and in actual battle they are the ones, along with the M.O. to whom the men look up.

Today's war accounts gave us a lot of encouragement. The Russians will soon be in Poland and the Eighth Army seems again to have the Germans on the run. Please God the end will soon be here and then we can be thinking of the quickest way home. The weather has changed the past few days for the best. I sure hope it continues to stay that way. One of the things in abundance here is fruit. I have eaten so many nuts that I feel like a monkey. Apples, oranges, figs, and olives are in great quantities.

Tonight we are having another Italian lesson. I know the alphabet and the vowels and a few common sentences. I'll be able to sing in Italian in the bathtub when I get back!

December 7, 1943.

Each day we are getting a lot of sunshine although the nights are very cold. I am continuing to see a lot of the Southern part of Italy. The hospitals I visit to see all my men are more or less spread around. I had a visit to Taranto a few days ago and was much impressed with the place. All the seaports are very attractive. So far no Christmas parcels have reached the Unit. It appears that we are going to have a lot of Christmas cheer all at once. We are already planning for our Christmas celebrations. There are many things such as fruit, fowl and candies that we could not get in England but can get here in abundance. The companies already have had a very good share of lamb and pork. One just has to go out to a farm with seven or eight hundred lira to purchase livestock.

Last night we had a wonderful Italian jazz band in to entertain the boys. All of them were great musicians although they had a time beating out some of our modern tunes. They go in for a lot of classical pieces but if you whistle the tune they have no trouble picking it up. The boys got a real kick out of them and so we have arranged to have them back. They play all night for 600 lira.

Right now we are continuing to push the Germans out of this country. From all accounts we have received it looks as though the final push is about to go into full swing.

December 14, 1943.

The light in my office is very dim and I'm having a time to get this written. Some evenings it goes up and down and sometimes it goes off altogether. Yesterday I spent most of my time in a city about 35 miles away looking up some of my men. I managed to find three of the six which is not so good. I'm afriad the hospital situation out here is going to drive me nutty. There seems to be no way of finding a man once he leaves. Possibly when we get all our own hospitals it may be different. Still I have lots of mail for the lads and I'm sure they would be glad to have it. I have been carrying around some of it for about three weeks. We seem to have a lot of lads down with colds and flu.

I met a number of the lads from the First Division. They seem to be a bright lot although they have been fighting hard for some time. I like their hopefulness and am banking on what they say about the end as being right. It looks very much like we will have to lick the German before he gives up.

I managed a few oranges for breakfast and that is a real treat since we never saw them in England. I understand they will be coming in greater quantities from now on since the harvest will be in full swing. I'm still seeing lots of the country. Today when I stopped my car I had a lot of children gathering around. They tend to be pesty but I can't get tough with them. I'd love to gather them up and take them somewhere where I could give them a real bath. Speaking of baths, last night I had a wonderful one. I waited for an hour for the water to warm up but it was worth it. The little Italian who runs the place is real comical. He thought that I should learn a few swear words so he threw a few at me. When he learned that I didn't make a habit of swearing he seemed surprised but replied that I'll need them here.

December 20, 1943.

Here we are five days from Christmas. The weather is more like spring and not at all like the real Canadian winter. There is nothing in the way of Christmas decorations in any of the towns. I had always thought that Italy was the one place where you would see all the colour and splendor of the festive season. I hardly think the war would change the situation. From what I can gather, they never have it. Despite our nearness to the front we are going to celebrate Christmas in the best Canadian tradition. I have Paul at the moment seeing if he can buy some coloured paper. I'm planning on decorating the mess halls and the tables. I am still worried about the Christmas parcels from home. If those in authority really know how morale is associated with the mail from home, they would never let it slip the way they have. Saturday, the Unit moved out on a scheme but I remained behind to clean up my hospital visitations. We were on the road to meet the men about six, and some of the country that we had to drive through was very tough. One spot on the journey took us over a range of mountains. We went straight up for about ten miles before reaching the top. I spent the day with the troops and since they were on the move, I couldn't hold any service. I left them after they had taken their final objective for the day.

This morning I was to go the hospital 40 miles away but having no mail for the boys prevented my journey. I will go tomorrow if any comes in today.

December 25, 1943.

It is 8:30 p.m. in Italy and our Christmas festivities are over. Everybody had a splendid time. I was up at 6:00 a.m., got to my office at 7:30 where I set up the PA system and before the men were out of bed I was playing Christmas carols. As the music wound its way up through the courtyard, I could see a window here and there being opened and a lot of sleepy men sticking their heads out wondering what was going on. Soon every window in the building was open and the men were singing with the records. This lasted till around 8:30 a.m. when we went off to breakfast. After breakfast I set up the PA again and played the records from home. This went over very well. When that was finished we held a carol service that took us to noon. We gathered in the mens' mess where they sat down to lots of turkey and plum pudding, wine, oranges, and nuts. Each man got 50 smokes as well. As usual the officers and sergeants waited tables and it was amusing to hear the lads calling for service. When they are 'top dog' they like to 'bark' a lot! Tonight we had our officers' dinner and it was tops. I ate turkey and pudding until I felt I would burst.

Unfortunately there is a little sadness thrown into our Christmas celebrations. Yesterday I buried out first lad in Italy. He was accidently shot on the evening of the 23rd. I wrote his mother in Chatham today, I'm sure it will be a real heartbreak for her. I know that many mothers are going through the same thing all the time. We gave him a real military funeral and that is sometimes most difficult to do under the conditions of the times.

The parcels for the men did not come and this was a real disappointment. They'll be just as welcome in the New Year. I do wish our Canadian officials would make a better effort and see that the mail gets to the troops. So many men said to me, "Padre, if only I had gotten a letter from home it would have made Christmas so much better." They get down in the mouth.

December 27, 1943.

Still no mail. I told some of the lads that if I didn't soon get a letter from my wife I would see the Padre to start an investigation. They all got a real laugh out of it. Well, the Christmas festivities are over for another year and I pray the last Christmas I have to put in in the army. Despite the absence of mail from home everyone seemed to have a good time. Yesterday I held my service in the local theatre. I had the Brigadier and General present and about 800 men. Everything went off well enough although the place was so packed it didn't seem like a very comfortable service for the troops. In the evening I conducted services in the local Protestant church and had about 90 men present. If these services continue to grow I don't know where I will put the lads. It's rather unusual to have so many on a voluntary basis. The Italian congregation sang a few carols for us. Many of the local people have lived in Canada and the States. Last night one of the men walked home with me. In 1933, he had spent a few months in Toronto. He asked me about places like Yonge Street, Eatons, Simpsons. It was like talking to a lad from home. When I asked him what brought him back to Italy he replied, "I really don't know."

Today I was busy in the local hospital. Tonight it is very cold but at least here we don't have to worry about blackouts. It seems funny now that we are so close that they don't insist on it. In England if you were caught with a light showing you would be put in prison. Here everything is just the opposite. I drive at night with all my lights on. I suppose the nearer you get to the real thing the less you have to worry. There is really nothing much the Germans don't know about this country so why bother being secretive. The news today was good on all fronts. We are still in the same spot and have no idea when our turn will come.

December 29, 1943.

The wonderful weather is not so wonderful anymore. It turned very cold and we have a bit of snow. Last night I literally froze in bed. We have no heat in our building and since all the floors are made of stone it does make a fellow shiver. It is hard to believe what one can put up with.

Yesterday I visited the hospital. It is about 40 miles away and since I had to climb over some very high mountains where the snow seems to find a good resting place, it was all the old car could do to make the grade. I hope when our turn comes for action, the weather will have changed.

I have had to deal with a few unhappy incidents these past few days. Yesterday morning I had a lad to see me who had received a letter from home saying his wife was in the hospital with cancer. He just broke down as he told me the story. I have applied for compassionate leave and the C.O. has concurred so I pray we may get him home before it is too late. The other was a lad whose brother had been killed with the First Division. They had planned to meet each other in a week or so. He wants to get up to the front so he can see the grave. War brings so many sorrows. I pray it will soon end.

December 31, 1943.

Confidence and not fear constrains me. To live to return is a daily certainty. I have an inner conviction that God wants me for further service and because of that He will see me through the present strife. Hopelessness and failure is the creed of the foolish and if a man's religion means anything at all, it should fill him with unbounded confidence in the psalm *'God is our refuge and strength.'* It just leads us forward and takes the fear out of danger, the hardships out of warfare and gives courage when timidity would make failures of us all. This sounds like a bit of a sermon but that's just the way I feel.

Tomorrow 1944 will be born. From all our new accounts it appears that we are now shaping up for the final assault. With all the new commands allocated, it looks as though the final drive will be made any day. It is interesting to speculate where it will take place. I think France will be the spearhead of the attack. It would be more interesting still to know how the Germans are considering our new offensive. One would assume before it began that they would seek some kind of peace. Their situation on every front is now hopeless and why they wish to continue to support failure is beyond me.

We still have no idea when we shall meet the Germans. Naturally it's in the order of things that our turn should soon come. One cannot live too long on or near the battlefield as we are and not come sooner or later to grips with the foe.

Tomorrow I lose Paul to the YMCA. He has been very faithful and has been with me nearly three years. I am sure going to miss him. I'm getting a lad by the name of Ted Reeves whom I know very well so it won't feel like a stranger in the midst.

Our Turn Has Now Arrived.

January 1, 1944.

This is a New Year's Day with lots of rain. It has rained all day and with the rain has come a very cold wind. You can hear it whistling through the open windows all over our building. I spent the morning visiting the men in hospital. Some mail has come through and that added much colour to my visits. We had many visitors in our mess from the various units. Many of our officers went out and around to pay the necessary compliments but my business in the hospitals kept me occupied throughout the day. We had a buffet lunch at noon and are laying on a turkey spread for supper.

Last night in the local theatre we had a concert for our men. Only half of the concert party turned up. Then, too, the electrical system was most irregular. It all tended to kill the spirit of the thing and had it not been for the fact that the English artists worked equally well in the darkness as in the light, it might have proved a complete flop. After the concert I was invited out to an Italian's home where I spent a very agreeable evening despite my lack of the language. On my way home I visited the sergeant's mess where most of the lads were having the time of their lives. I started a new diary today. I was just looking over my record of New Year's Day 1943 in Aldershot, England. I noticed the day was wet and cold with a few snow flurries.

January 3, 1944.

It is just 9:00 in Italy. Out of my office window I can see one of the finest moons I have ever seen. Yesterday I had a busy day. We filled the local theatre with troops at 10:45 a.m. and I gave them a New Year's message. I took for my text PHILLIP 3: 13-14: 'This one thing I do, forgetting those things which are behind and reaching forth to those things which are before. I press toward the mark for the prize.' It made a very suggestive New Year's message. I hope it did some good. Last night I conducted the service in the local Protestant church and once again the place was packed to the doors. I conducted a communion service afterwards and all the men remained. The local congregation was on hand and since it's still close to the Christmas season the church decorations were still up. It made a nice setting for our service, and some of the men who had been there for the first time, told me afterwards that it reminded them of their home churches in Canada. Corporal Vendetti was there so I had him wish the congregation a Happy New Year from the men of the Canadian Army.

Any day now the big push should be on. I suppose we will be in it. Still, I feel Germany, when she realizes what's coming, will be quick to decide her policy and seek some kind of peace. Everyone out here feels that this is the year that will bring the end. Some feel that it will be over by early spring.

January 5, 1944.

The lights just went out again. What a country! Guess I'll have to find a candle to keep this going. News has just come in that the Russians are in Poland, I shouldn't wonder but the German 'goose' is cooked on that front. It is great news and I'm sure it will be well received by all. Last night I went to the local theatre. It was Irish night and of course the whole Unit was present. We saw 'My Sister Eileen'. Since I hadn't seen it before I more than enjoyed it.

I had a discussion group with the men today and at the end we had a talk about our attitude toward things in Canada when we return. Some of the boys have strange ideas on the subject but all agree that going home will more than compensate for any differences that may be prevalent in our lives. Today it was just like Canadian weather – snow and more snow. We have now a few inches. It's very cold as well but unlike Canada in that we have no way to keep ourselves warm.

January 7, 1944.

Living in Italy and seeing as we do, the awful conditions that prevail, accentuates the prayers that our families are spared the devastating plague of war. It leaves so many vulgar marks upon men, women and children. Only true peace will cure the sadness that this scene paints. It makes me happy when I know that the fury of war will be unknown in Canada, save for the sorrow in the loss of so many of our fine young Canadians. That sadness will be felt in many homes. The end we all believe, is near. There is rising daily among us, an optimism so real and vital that already we are talking about our return trip to dear old Canada!

We have had a lot of snow along with some rain and cold which none of us enjoy. I've dreaded going into my room at night for it's like going into a refrigerator. I usually take a lot of time getting out of my clothes. I go through all kinds of stunts before I get into my bedroll. It takes a long time to warm up.

Today I visited the hospital to see one of the men who got into a very bad car accident. Poor lad is pretty low although the doctor assured me that he would make the grade. I had a number of letters from his wife which I read to him, but he was so sick he didn't seem too interested. Since he has both arms broken he will be unable to write so I have dropped off a letter to his wife. I'm sure that she will worry.

January 15, 1944.

I'm writing this letter under strange and new conditions. If my writing seems to be shaky here and there you will know it's the vibration of guns going off all around me. I suppose when one gets used to it there is little to upset the thinking mind. I had the pleasure of meeting a couple of padres yesterday who have been in the lines for some time and naturally I hear some strange stories. I knew one of them in England and when I saw him I hardly recognized him. He has been working pretty hard and as a result he is getting run down.

Yesterday Bill Elder and I went off to get some mules. What a job! The mules must have known we were green for they cut-up for fare and I thought more than once, that they would kick the pants off both of us. After some time we managed to get them into our area but it was some job. The mules are used for hauling rations and since this country is very hilly only this kind of animal can make the grade. One of these days when I become an expert I will get my picture taken on one.

So far things are going very well and everybody seems calm and confident. I have an idea that we will do all that is expected and more. When the Hun sees an Irishman coming his way he will head for home! I hope right away! From all accounts the padres have a 24 hour job. While I'm writing this letter there is a lot of fire going over my head, which to say the least is very annoying.

I've got a call from our hospital. Our first casualty has come in.

January 17, 1944.

I'm having a very busy time. I'm working with the M.O. and am crowded into a very small house for which the Hun has no respect. Casualties come in night and day hence resting and sleeping are a bit out of order. I try to keep lots of warm tea on hand and no matter how badly the lads feel, they go for it in a big way. Our men are standing up well and feel more than equal to the task. Once they get the first few days over they will settle in. I was up forward seeing some of the boys this morning and ran into Padre Crawford Smith. He has been very busy and was exhausted so I brought him back for some tea. This is proving quite the experience for us.

I didn't have any service yesterday. I guess they will be out for a while. The most I can do is go around and see the lads and when anything happens to comfort them and bring them a little cheer. So far no parcels or mail have reached us in our new positions. When we get out for a rest we will have a grand time reading our letters and getting some off.

The past few days have been tough going. Not being able to get a sleep or a wash makes the old system a little rebellious. I was out this morning looking for one of my lads who was killed. I came to a little town or what was once a town, and ran into Padre Goforth. Apparently the lad was taken into his area and he had buried him. I put a cross on his grave and left him in peace among the Italian hills.

January 19, 1944.

Today we are having a bit of a rest and I can tell you it does feel good. I had a wonderful night's sleep and when I got up there was a lovely sun shining. It made me feel as if there was nothing the matter in this world. My day began in a perfect way. Ted, my batman, brought me a lot of mail from home. It is certainly a real stimulant for a lonely heart. About an hour ago I had a wonderful wash and change of clothes. Ted cut down a gasoline tin and filled it with warm water so I spread a canvas out on the ground and went at it right out in the open. The sun was hot so there was nothing to endure. I can say that I will be satisfied with little when I do get back home.

I had to write a letter to the sister of the lad who was killed and that is always a hard job for me. I'm indeed thankful that we got off lightly and trust that good fortune will continue to follow us as we go further into this business. The picture we get of the battle is rather limited but we do hear that things on the whole are going well. I haven't heard any war news for about a week so I don't know at the moment how things stand. I do know that our men are confident and have no fear of the Germans and that all adds to our successes. The pounding we give them before we go in makes one wonder how anyone can live under it. I know that they are pretty well shaken for when prisoners are taken they appear to be '*punch-drunk*' from all the shelling.

Now that I have tasted a bit of the business I know that I will be all right. There is naturally a lot of work for me but with the help of God I can manage. I have already learned the art of ducking when the big stuff comes over. One of the funniest things to happen to me (although it wasn't humorous at the time) occurred when I had reason to go out to '*check the plumbing*'. The Germans started dropping mortars around. A few pieces came my way and up I got in a hurry and ran with my pants around my knees for cover. It was a most embarrassing situation. That was one time when I was really caught with them down!

January 20, 1944.

I am writing this letter outside under a very hot sun. If it keeps up I should get it finished before dark. I have had many lads to see me during the day. They seem to come and go with their problems all the time. Now that we are in the front lines there are new ones emerging.

Things don't move so quickly here and you would understand the reason if you saw the country we have to fight in. It's all mountains and just pushing Jerry from one to the other takes all our time. He can dig in and has the advantage until we reach him. Getting to him is sometimes a real tough go. Had the terrain been like the desert we would have had him out of here long ago.

Some mail clippings of our arrival have come in to the lads and I have just looked at my picture. It is one that was taken at a sports meet while we were in Debert. I look more like a high-priced bookie than a padre!

January 24, 1944.

If war does nothing else it certainly places one in some odd situations. The dear old Rockies have nothing on my present location. The view one gets reminds me now and then of some Canadian scenery. I am attached to the R.A.P. but am pleased to report that we have little to do.

The mud is terrible and it sticks like glue. I gathered a few Italians together this morning and got them to dig out a new road for us. I think I should have been in the Engineers for my effort was superb! So far we have had it easy but since you have to stand ready for action it keeps you primed up. I get a lot of letters to censor so that helps to fill in some of my time. The lads are so security-minded that there is precious little one has to erase.

Today I had the opportunity to visit some of the lads in their positions. The mud is so bad that there are times when it just seems to come in around your posterior. By the time I got back to my post, I was leg weary and very tired. Guess I'm getting too old for all this activity. The lads were all in good spirits and pleased to see me. All tell me that I have no need to remind them to pray for they're at it constantly. Conditions are such that it makes a man think. One lad, in a very serious mood, told me that he "prays like hell" all the time. We are gradually making the Hun give ground. Our casualties remain light and I pray they continue that way. I am feeling fine and am managing to carry out my responsibilities with diligence and care.

January 27, 1944.

Things are a bit tough at the moment and I hope it eases up before long. We are having a lot of rain and it makes our fighting most difficult. By the time I got in after doing what I had to do, I was covered from head to foot with mud. I gave myself a complete change and then got word that I had to go out and do the same thing again. Ah, 'tis some life being an army padre!

I trust that this war will be brought to an end quickly. When you see so many of our young lads being wounded it's not a very pleasant experience. I have been on the go night and day this past week. However, I'm very well and despite some of my night adventures, that sometimes get a little hot, I do feel that I'm doing something very worthwhile. Prior to this, my labours were child's play.

Today I had a number of refugees around my truck—mostly women and children. They come through the front line and it would break your heart just to see them. I had some candies which I gave the children and they could hardly wait for me to open the bag. They just about ate my hands off to get at them. War is hell and it is hell to be in the midst of it. I have to go out tonight to bury a lad. Since it has been a bright day some of the mud may have cleared. I am looking after myself and I'm not taking any chances.

January 29, 1944.

I have just returned from a very busy night following a full day. In less than an hour I'll be moving off again with a convoy of mules and if any of them get stuck tonight I'm going to take the load myself and leave them behind.

From the standpoint of weather, the day has just been about perfect. Since there was no way to hold church services, I undertook to give myself a bit of a clean up. I managed to score an overdue bath (open-air touch) followed by a complete change of clothes. After living one whole week in the same outfit you can imagine how I welcome a change. I was out again last night to bury one of my lads. I got through very well. The Hun must know who I am now for he left me completely alone. This is a dreadful business. Too bad our civilization hasn't been able to solve their international problems without war. I pause now and then midst all the noise and ask myself where we are headed and what we have accomplished.

A week in the lines has brought us some casualties but leaves the men more determined than ever to keep pushing the Hun back. I think we have now gotten over our battle fear. The men move to their duties with more ease. I've been scared plenty of times and often I have looked like dear old Pluto in the movies. You know how he digs himself under the ground – well that's me!

January 31, 1944.

I'm having an easy night ... the first in six. I haven't had to go out and have appreciated the rest. All day I have been busy taking care of the personal effects of our killed and writing next-of-kin letters. I find that part of my work the most distressing for it brings out too forceably the horror of war.

We experienced another wonderful day and it now looks like we are in for some fine weather. The Italians tell us that spring starts tomorrow. I hope for our sakes that they are right. If only we could get this awful mud dried up we could go places in a hurry.

Our lads are standing up very well and considering the difficulties under which they fight I think they are wonderful. We have a little Italian boy living in our R.A.P. and he is picking up the English "lingo". Each morning he comes in and has breakfast with us. The lads gave him a haircut and wash today and he now looks like a wee Canadian.

The dear old Jerry is now throwing over some shells so I'm off to safer quarters.

February 1, 1944.

I had my first free night since coming into the line. We didn't have a casualty of any kind and so for today we have a clean medical sheet. I had an opportunity to visit the companies this afternoon and I wish I could relate all the stories they had to tell. While there is a grimness to war, comedy does enter the scene now and again and gives much colour to some of the exploits.

This is supposed to be the first day of spring but the way the sun behaved you would think that it was the middle of summer. If only there was no war a man could really enjoy his surroundings. Most of our mud holes have dried up and that in itself is a blessing. Every little bit helps to brighten life. I've been sleeping in a truck and using a bedroll for so long now it will be grand to throw the whole thing overboard and get back to civilization.

February 6, 1944.

I came out of the line on Friday and spent most of the day at our rear position gathering up mail and equipment for the lads in the hospitals. I started out on my trip early Saturday morning and since the day was wet and cold, it was tough driving. I got as far as Foggia last night where Ted and I just pulled in by the side of the road, and after a meal bedded down for the night. This morning as we ate breakfast an old Italian lady dropped in. She was hungry and cold, so we fed her. I never saw food disappear so quickly. These people are just starving.

I got to the hospital about noon and went right to work. I finished about eight at night and stayed over. I do feel very deeply for our wounded. All seem very bright and I'm glad they have the mail and parcels. I know it helps a lot.

February 11, 1944.

My present location is the barest I have yet struck. Not long ago the Germans were in possession of this town and naturally what is left you could put in a good size bag. Our lads had to do a bit of pounding to get them out. In any case I am in place tonight, and since we are out of the lines after a month of fighting we can't complain too much.

I have just finished speaking to a very interesting Italian fellow. He lived in New York for a good number of years, so speaks English quite well. He was saying that when the war is over he is going back. I asked him why he returned in the first place, and he told me that he came home to marry the girl he loved and Mussolini got him. I wish I could relate all that he told me.

Suffice it to say that the Germans stole everything they had. I'm afraid the war has brought out the very worst in man. The brotherhood of man at the moment, is but a dream.

February 13, 1944.

All day I had a steady stream of lads, including officers, to my one-room house. I think they like the big log fire I keep burning and the tea that Ted always keeps brewing. This morning I had a volunteer church service and had around 300 of the lads present. I held the service in a bombed out Catholic church. It's the only building standing in this town so we took it over. Funny what the fortunes of war create. I don't think we can do much from where we are until the weather dries up. The most we can do is hold the line and worry Jerry with patrolling. I do wish the darn thing would end right away.

February 15, 1944.

I'm entertaining tonight. It's pretty muddy and cold outside so I have a grand fire going and everyone is enjoying the hospitality that my little Italian room can afford. Ted is passing out shortbread and Christmas cake to complete the picture. We talked a lot about what will happen to the soldier when this is over.

It's now the middle of the month and we are told that the weather won't be with us for another four weeks. All of this means that we will be standing still. We have enjoyed our rest period and will be in much better spirits going back into the line. This morning I was busy with 'Padre's Hour'. After a month in the line the lads had a lot of interesting questions to ask. This afternoon a very good band came into our area and gave us a couple of hours of fine music. The leader of the group was a Mr. Murphy from Dublin. You can guess how well we hit it off!

February 16, 1944.

Tonight I write from a new area. Our rest period is over. I have again struck a very good house in which to make my abode. The M.O. is living with me and since we are an agreeable pair it looks as if our stay in this spot will be o.k. We went out in a very heavy snowstorm and cut enough logs to last us for a few days. While we were out, Ted prepared an excellent supper for us. He found a small tablecloth and had it all fixed, up so when we came to sit down to eat, it added a real touch of home. He did so well that we are now calling him Mrs. Reeves. I must add that he has been terrific through it all.

February 17, 1944.

This has not been a very exciting day. The M.O. got up this morning but had to go back to bed. He is quite sick, but we are taking good care of him. I was out today seeing some of the lads. I found one company living in slit-trenches half full of water. I sometimes wonder why men have to suffer so. These conditions are terrible. As I went from one trench to the other, I found men smiling and joking. They sure know how to turn the worst into the best. One lad said "Padre, when I get home this will help me to appreciate a good bed with white sheets."

This morning I came across a young Italian lad around 17. He was hungry and cold so I took him in and attended to his needs. He then went off and in a little while came back with fresh cut logs for the fire. I gave him a few smokes as I certainly appreciated his efforts.

The mud is now in liquid form. It not only sticks but runs all over the place. We are wallowing in it just like the pigs. I have two pair of boots and while I have to change a couple of times a day, I'm still much better off than most.

We haven't had any war news for a long time so really don't know how things are going. The mortars have been pounding in and we have suffered a few casualties.

February 20, 1944.

Being Sunday I managed to get three services in. We can't have church parades any more. I just have about 20 or 30 lads in a quiet spot in the line and hold a short service. Sometimes they are cut off fast but today we had no outside interference. The day was cold and wet and the mud is still with us. We are alive and well, have plenty to eat, so we have little to complain about. I had two most appreciative letters in reply to next-of-kin letters that I sent back to Canada. The poor mothers do take their sorrow heroically. My heart goes out to them.

It has been very quiet and we pray it will last. I'm feeling pretty well and since I have the M.O. living with me, I should be well cared for.

February 23, 1944.

I am happy to report that last night was indeed a quiet one. We didn't get out of our bedroll and that is a first for a few weeks.

Today was another quiet day. Possible the weather is about to break and turn in our favour. One of my Italian friends told me that when the sun comes out in Italy it burns '*like hellie*'. I only hope I got the truth from him as I passed it on to a good many. No matter how small or how insignificant the news is, we pass it on, and the funny thing is that it seems to have a good effect. Rumours of course, go the rounds here just as they did back home. One of the most common questions I get when I'm making my rounds is, "Padre, when are we going back to Canada?"

I saw a paper today. The first in ages. Everything seems to be going well in our favour. The terrific bombing that Germany is getting night and day should help to soften the road for us. I think I'm getting very hard and callous. War does funny things to all of us. It is terrible how hostile we become.

February 25, 1944.

This has been another quiet day. As far as my department is concerned the past few days have been perfect. I'm beginning to wonder if I'm really in the front line. It rained all day and has spoiled our notion about getting a break in the weather.

We have a bit of a rest centre opened up and I'm in charge. I make my rounds a couple of times a day to see the lads. All of them receive food on coming in, so are stocked up with good things to eat. I have four Italian civilians working as 'fatigue men' and they do a good job. They too score on the men's parcels, as the lads treat them well. They are as scared as the deuce when Jerry starts dropping his 'eggs'. A couple of them passed me this afternoon and the way they were going, I thought one of our lads was after them with a gun. It was just a few close mortars.

February 26, 1944.

The night is very dark, damp and cold. We had a new M.O. come in as a relief for Captain Bolley. Things still remain very quiet and that is very agreeable to me. I just hope it continues.

We no longer hold regular Sunday services. I just get a few men together in small groups where I can. Today I managed two communions as well. The lads have been asking for services which is rather an unusual occurrence. The services have continued to be on a voluntary basis. I would rather have twenty men come on their own than have the whole Unit paraded for compulsory services. One lad told me after the service tonight that the reason he was there was because he was not ordered to come. I really get a big kick out of things the way they are now, even though, as was the case this morning, I had to out-shout Jerry to make myself heard.

February 28, 1944.

For the first time in many a long day we had the sun shine on us with all its power. It was so strong that we took our clothes and hung them all over the place. I went back this morning to what we call out 'B' echelon and conducted a service. The men are now so widely spread, that I can't cover them all on Sundays, so I just have a service any day of the week. The lads seem to welcome it.

The days are beginning to lengthen in this part of the world. I noticed it wasn't dark until around 6:30 p.m. We had another good night and I didn't have to move out of my sleep. If this continues I'm afraid that I'll be getting 'front-line spoiled'.

The lads are now getting eight days leave. You should see how happy they are when they start off. Officers also are included. When my turn comes I really don't have any idea where I will go.

February 29, 1944.

Everyone feels that with the coming of the good weather will come the end of the Hun in Italy. We have had another good day today. The sun gave us its best. Already the roads and fields are drying up.

I had a busy day and had several tasks to perform which I did not relish. I buried a couple of English soldiers who we found in our area. They had been dead for a couple of months. Needless to say, it wasn't a pleasant experience.

I spent some time with the lads at the *'Padre's Rest Centre'* which they now call it. I worked in a *'Padre's Hour'* and distributed parcels that had been turned over to me for the men who have been killed.

March 1, 1944.

This has been a quiet day. Last night we were very busy so I didn't get the rest and sleep I'm accustomed to. There was nothing very serious and that indeed makes me happy. It does hurt to see lads who I know so well coming through badly wounded.

I was off on a chaplain's course today and met all the chaplains. It's been a long time since we had a chance to get together. The over forty are being pulled back from front line units to hospitals. I'm glad it doesn't affect me since I wouldn't want to leave the Irish.

The weather continues to be splendid and the sun is giving off scorching heat.

March 5, 1944.

This was a very wet Sunday evening and I'm now waiting for 7:30 to put on a service for 20 or 30 of the lads who are located in an old Italian house just a little distance away.

Our services are not large but somehow they are made much more helpful in that all come with a willing heart and enter right into the spirit of it. This morning I managed a service for one of the companies and had well over half of them present. Considering some of the natural difficulties, it went through without interference.

It has already started to rain again and the mud is about to play havoc with us.

Out of the Line ... Rest Period

March 7, 1944.

Yesterday I left the front line along with some others for a new area. I was on the road all day. When we arrived here we were tired and after a cup of tea, went to bed. I was up early this morning and went off with George Duncan to look over our new abode.

It is far from the noise of the guns. As a matter of fact it seems odd not hearing shells coming and going. This part of the country has missed the war. Everything is intact. The people seem to be more full of their own importance. If you wanted a house up around the front, you just took it. Here you have to plead for it and then perhaps not get it. I can't quite figure these people out. You'd think they would be out to help us but they seem very indifferent.

The country is mostly farmland and at the present time the orchards are out in full bloom. It is in marked contrast to the filth evident in the towns and villages.

March 8, 1944.

Tonight I am trying to make myself comfortable in an old Italian farmhouse. There is no fireplace but I have plenty of blankets in my bedroll so I won't be cold. The day was chilly and wet and spring is showing itself in the fields and on the trees.

We are waiting for the remainder of the Unit to come in. I came on the advance party. I know the lads will like it around here. There is no sign of war.

Tonight the farmers where we are staying had George Duncan and I in for supper. It's a bit difficult to describe the setting. There were about a dozen men, women and children present. Everyone sat around a large table and ate and ate. The only thing I recognized was chicken. While the meal was going on the small baby had to have his so mother just obliged him at the table. I think the baby had a better meal than the rest of us! They couldn't understand why I didn't drink their wine. I had to explain, so to make it easy I told them I had a bad stomach. That made them all sorry for me and away they went to bring me something for my 'ailment'. When no one was looking I poured it under the table.

Things are going fine at the moment. It's wonderful to be out of the lines. My heart just about breaks when I see our lads come in wounded or when I'm called on to bury them. The news of our casualties will be filtering back each day.

March 11, 1944.

For the first time in four days the sun is actually shining. Since the lads had come out of the line for a rest, I was hoping they would get a little bit of comfort – they deserve it. I was around the companies this afternoon and it was wonderful the change a bit of sunshine had made in all of them.

It is now a week since I have seen a newspaper so I don't know how things on the war front are going. I feel that this summer should see us through. Right now, I find myself crowded in a little Italian room with ten other officers. Everybody is smoking and generally talking about the goings on. Tomorrow morning I'm leaving on a tour of the hospitals. I will cover about 500 miles. I have a lot of mail and parcels so I should be a welcome guest. I heard today that three of our officers who were wounded will be going back to Canada. I'm hoping to catch them before they leave. As usual we are having an interesting time with the local Italian farmers. They won't take money for their eggs or chickens. They want to barter. I had an old shirt that I exchanged for a nice cooked chicken; one pair of socks is good for a dozen eggs. I should say that despite the conditions we are eating well.

March 15, 1944.

Today I was very busy contacting our reinforcements. I met all the lads just over from Canada. They look a good lot and should be a real help to us. I got through a couple of hospitals and finished up the day around supper time. My trip so far (and I'm just half-way through) has been very worthwhile. I can say that I have never met men more anxious to see me and have a talk. Some I know I won't see again until I get back home; others will return to the Unit when they are better. I have three more hospitals to visit. It will take me a day to reach them and another to visit the patients.

I arrived back in camp this afternoon around four, after completing a 450 mile visit to our lads in the hospitals. If you have a map of Italy and draw a line from Ortona to Naples over the heights and snow of the Apennines, through the planes of Foggia, it will give a fair idea of the trip I have just completed. I visited seven hospitals and saw 135 men. It was a most successful trip and I hope I left the lads just a wee bit happier. A list of the casualties has been sent home. It's a bit grim to see all these lads coming in. I don't relish my job at times. I had replies from several of the wives and mothers. Their letters are so full of grief and sorrow it's a bit hard to get through them. All were most appreciative of what I had done.

I had a service for the lads today and sang for our opening hymn '*Unto the Hills*' ... most appropriate for our surroundings.

March 20, 1944.

I'm sitting in the back of my truck as I write. It's just about 5:00 p.m. and another good day is coming to a close. The ground has dried up and right now you can drive anywhere without getting stuck.

I attended a chaplain's meeting this morning where we got a new army order giving permission to troops to marry in this country! We all thought it a bit of a joke. I'm not sure any of our lads has marriage on his mind just now. I'm not certain how long we will remain here. My guess is until the good weather is a certainty and then along with the rest, we will join in on a drive. If we can get the Germans on the run it shouldn't take too long to finish it off. If the allies can get Finland and Rumania out, I should think that the remainder of the Balkan countries will follow. It's now shaping up for something really big.

March 26, 1944.

I am writing this in front of my truck with the engine running so I can keep warm. This morning I drove over to another unit to conduct a service. The lads all crowded into a small hut which I thought would blow over before I got finished. I'm not convinced that religion under such unfavourable circumstances goes down very well. When I got back to my own lines I couldn't see asking the men to stand out in the open while I expounded on the mysteries of the Kingdom. I just called the whole thing off. It is really going to be something when I preach from behind a pulpit again. It is going to take me some time to become *'minister conscious'* again. Most of the time I no more look like a clergyman than some of the Italian farmers!

March 27, 1944.

I spent my morning in a nearby hospital where I found about a dozen of the lads. They're just in with flu and bad colds. The conditions have been severe under canvas, hence a number get sick. After going through this experience I should be the perfect gypsy by the time I get home. I find I can be comfortable in a truck and despite my cramped quarters, manage very well. Tonight Bill Elder and I have been elected to defend the honour of the Irish in a bridge game with another unit in the Brigade. If systems lend strength to victory we have many worked out. He's been dropping in all day reminding me what I'm to do when he bids a certain way. It will put the night in out here and that alone is a real accomplishment.

March 28, 1944.

Bill and I emerged the victors by 2500 points! We had a good feed and got back to our area around noon. This morning I didn't feel much like getting up but did make it around light. Sleeping in my truck has this advantage: no one knows when you do get up or go to bed.

I'm getting a new truck, a 15 cwt. It's a bit longer and of course I can always use more room. I seem to gather up so much stuff as I go along. I really don't know what I'm going to do with it when the end comes. Things seem to be very quiet ... perhaps the lull before the storm. There should be a lot of fireworks any day.

We had the mobile baths in today and we all treated ourselves. I must say it is funny the things you do in the army. We have this compensation: that it's the only place in the world we will have to do it in. After the movie tonight Bill Elder invited me over to his tent. In came his batman with a big roasted chicken. We didn't have any utensils so we went at it with our hands and believe me we made short work of it. Often Bill comes over to my truck in the evening for a cup of tea and something to eat. Sometimes it's not much but often it's a well-fried egg. You see we are not doing too badly after all.

April 1, 1944.

It's just about 8:00 p.m. and still quite light. The clocks were moved forward one hour at midnight. The dark shades of evening are just beginning to come down upon the high mountains and here and there you can see a flicker of light reflecting off small pockets of snow.

Today was about the warmest we've had. The lads were going around in their sleeves. I held my first service for the Princess Louise at 8:45 a.m. and had about 300 of the boys present. On the way back we just got to a little town when the R.C. church service was coming out. Being Palm Sunday everybody was carrying huge sprays of olive branches. As we passed by, all the children ran upon our jeep and graciously waved the branches over us. When I got to the other side of town I found water running down my face. I had my service for our lads at 10:45 and had a great turnout.

This evening the Italian family on whose farm we are staying invited us all for supper. I didn't go but in a little while one of the officers came back to tell me that the people wanted the "grey-haired captain" to come. It sure made me feel old.

The activity around the camp is very quiet. We never thought that we would get so long to rest and I hear it will last for another week or so. This evening we saw the movie "His Favourite Wife". I never laughed so much or so hard. The story was very true-to-life and me thinks will occur plenty after the war!

April 7, 1944.

This is Good Friday but unfortunately we were unable to observe the day. The troops left very early this morning on a scheme. I had other things to do so didn't go. I drove out this evening with Bill Leonard to see the boys and have just arrived back.

This afternoon Bill Elder and I went into town to have our hair cut. Well, I think we got the laugh of our lives. The barber, who could speak a little English, had his two sons working with him. One who was just 12, cut Bill's hair and made an excellent job of it. The other, who was 9, worked on the shaving end of the affair. I never did see such a perfect combination.

Ted painted the truck and gave it a regular going over. I did a little painting myself. I'm well supplied with transport with the truck and a jeep. The officials think we can get around a lot better with a jeep in the front lines.

April 8, 1944.

The lads have come in from their scheme. They certainly look a tired lot. We seem cut off from everything in this area. Right now I don't know how the war is going. A few days ago I did hear that the Russians were making fine progress in Rumania. One of these days we will hear that they have reached Germany. The mail is awfully slow. Our Canadian postal officials should get a kick in the pants. Under these favourable conditions there is no reason why they can't make a better effort.

We Are Back in the Line

April 10, 1944.

Yesterday we were on the road all day and didn't get into our new area until quite late. It's beginning to look like our rest period is over. We've had a good one so have no room to complain.

Today it was raining '*cats and dogs*' and our new area is not so good. We are again having problems with our famous Italian mud. I held my Easter service and had 450 lads present. I got them on a side of a hill, close to a town taken not so long ago by the Canadians. When the local inhabitants heard the pipe band they all came rushing out to see what was going on. Believe it or not they hung around for the entire service. It was a splendid morning and that helped a great deal.

I am out in the open as I write. On every side there are mountains. Indeed, we are completely shut in. I would say that they rise up about 3000 feet with the clouds resting in their fluffy whiteness, right on the top. The valley in which we are located was once a riverbed. They call this the front line but to find a German me thinks is going to be one tough job. The only indication of battle is the constant sound of the guns at a distance. If anything, the mountains inspire confidence for they are grand protectors.

We were on the road all day yesterday and didn't get into the line until 1:00 p.m. I had to leave Ted behind with my 8 cwt at a rear position and I came in with my jeep. For a while I'll have to act as my own batman. On my way in last night I saw my first plane shot down. It just seemed to drop like a dead bird right on top of the mountains. It is a shame that we can't find some way to settle our problems besides killing one another.

April 14, 1944.

My morning was taken up conducting '*Padre's Hour*'. It was quite a new experience the way we had to carry them out. We just gathered around a big rock and hoped no one above us would kick any loose dirt or stones down. Fortunately we got through without incident. I think the only thing that disturbed us was the sound of gun fire. The mountains have a way of making it seem worse than it really is.

We had one very hot day today and my face is as red as a berry. This afternoon I conducted six services and am now well talked out. The battalion positions are high up in the mountains so I went from one company to the other and got along famously. It sometimes seems quite strange holding a religious service when not so far away so many unchristian things are happening.

Today our lads are getting by without injury. This is the kind of warfare that I like.

April 17, 1944.

I am a long way from the front line tonight. I left the forward position early this morning in my jeep and headed south. The lads have a lot of needs such as writing paper, cards, crib boards, reading materials so I'm out on the scrounge. I'm sorry to say that our Y.M.C.A. auxiliary services are not everything one would desire. It seems that we have to keep chasing them. On the other hand the "Sally Ann" is right in the line with everything. They are tops with the boys. At times I wish the Church was as useful and as aggressive.

We are wondering these days when the big push will come.

April 19, 1944.

I've just seen the newspaper clippings about the padres. Yes, they are showing up very well. I'm not so sure I will ever accomplish such brave deeds. I'm too careful. Army decorations have no appeal to me. All I want to do is to carry out my job faithfully and well and return home as soon as this is over.

It's Sunday but just another day in the life of the soldier. The lads not far away from me in the slit trenches are now so well up on their prayers, they don't need any last minute spiritual guidance. Services of course are out of the question. I don't think Jerry would stop his shelling just to let us do a little worshipping.

I heard a rumour that we may be getting a breather tonight. The boys at the moment are preparing a nice roast. A young calf was killed in the shelling quite close to us, so we managed to get it and work on it before anything serious set in. If it tastes as good as it smells, it will be a great feast. I do think that we eat better in the line than out of it. Our hens had enough eggs laid before breakfast to give us all one apiece.

I often wonder what it will be like when I get back to my ministerial duties. The things I once thought important have faded into insigificance. When one sees the Church at a distance, it's not hard to discover the many non-essentials that clutter it up.

We have set up our R.A.P. in a rather unusual Italian house. The house looked very ordinary but when we got inside, we found that whoever owned it was rather well off as it was furnished elaborately. Since it sits in the middle of our advance, most of its contents have been badly shelled. The livestock are still around and we have a few hens that keep us supplied with fresh eggs. The boys are caring for them in grand style.

Today things have eased up a bit. I don't like to see any of our lads coming in wounded. We are hoping for a short break. The pace has been fast over very difficult country.

We hear little of what is going on in the outside world. Still we are hoping and praying the success already attained in France will hasten the end. With the number of casualties inflicted recently on the Hun, one wonders how he could manage to hang on much longer.

April 22, 1944.

I have been looking for a while at a very high mountain, not too far away. On it are our enemies. I suppose they can see us but as I looked I couldn't help but feel what a useless pursuit men strive for to solve their problems. I wouldn't wonder but the old mountain that has been there for centuries, has looked down before upon men and armies as they chased each other up and down her rugged sides. Maybe if the old mountain had a tongue she could give us all a lesson on the futility of war.

Yesterday I laid away two of my boys. One was twenty, the other twenty-two. One of the lads was married and waiting for mail to tell him he was a father. It is very tragic.

All mail has been cut off to the Free State. If DeValera doesn't smarten up all his people will starve. I can't see how they can live without the assistance of Britain and the U.S.A. It's a cinch that Germany won't come to his rescue. I think after the war I will have to go back and straighten out things in 'me own land.'

April 24, 1944.

We moved into a new spot in the line and we had some fun finding our way in the dark. We have a rather strange situation here. You have to stay under cover all day ... no movement of any kind is permitted. We are under the keen eye of the Jerry and if he sees movement, down comes his fire power. We have turned day into night. The M.O. and I have a house on the side of the mountain. We can look down into a narrow valley covered wlth all kinds of vegetation. All around we can see many pockets where hard battles are still going on.

Last night about 8:oo p.m. I had to go out to bury one of our lads. When I say that I got to where he was around midnight, it will give some idea of the distance I had to cover. By the time we get out of this position we should all be akin to mountain goats. It was a wonderful starry night and as I committed the poor lad to his last resting place, a bird in a tree commenced singing, almost as if in sympathy with what we were doing. When I got back I was called to bury one of the lads from our sister regiment but this was close to where I live, so I laid him away around 2:3o a.m.

The real problem at this point is how we are ever going to get the wounded back to the R.A.P.

April 26, 1944.

It's about 1:oo p.m. and the M.O. and I have just finished a hardtack dinner but we still are hungry. Because of our position we are unable to get the fresh rations. I'm sure by the time we leave this spot I'll be minus a few pounds and will look like a bully-beef tin. We mustn't complain too much for on the whole our food over here has been quite good.

We had another night free from casualties. Thank God! The M.O. and I didn't get up until around 10:oo a.m. Since we have to stay indoors all day, it matters little when you do make the scene. It's raining quite hard today. The first we have had in a long time. Since rocks don't make mud we won't suffer too much. I had a number of letters from our wounded lads who are now in England on their way back to Canada. All seem happy and content even though some are badly wounded.

It's getting close to the end of another month. Believe it or not we haVe been seven months in this country. We haven't any news since coming in so have really no idea how the war is going. At least we are doing our own little bit here and that contributes some to the war picture as a whole.

Last evening I decided to go out and visit some of the companies. It was a bad night to pick especially since it is difficult finding your way through bush and rock. It was so dark. I never did see such a black night. I got lost and had one time finding my way back to my hideout. At one point I walked right up to my knees into a river. Say, mountain water is cold!

The casualty picture remains pretty good. If a man gets wounded up here it's an awful business to get him back.

April 28, 1944.

It would appear, from the precautionary measures now in existence in England, that something must be doing. Just last night I heard that no one could leave the British Isles after midnight on the 27th. They certainly can't bank on winning the war here. It would take years to drive an army out of this country. You have only to see the place to realize the difficulty.

Last night Bill Armstrong and I headed out around 2:00 a.m. to call on Payne and Elder of 'B' company. We weren't very sure of their position, so we kept walking and climbing until we came upon some of their men. When we told them how we had come they could hardly believe it. Apparently we had walked through a mine field, right past the nose of the Hun. Guess Jerry was asleep. We finally reached out destination and after a short visit left for home. At one point on our return we came to a small valley with a river running through it. We couldn't find a way over it so we waded through it. It wasn't very deep. When I got back to the R.A.P. I found the M.O. sitting up looking quite worried. I like to get around to see the lads and I enjoy my night walks, falls and tumbles.

We had another night free from casualties. My it's wonderful the way we are getting through. Of course, we have had enough so far to last us while we are here.

Today the M.O. and I decided to visit a nearby Italian cemetery. It proved to be quite an experience. It had been badly shelled and many of the buried had been disinterred as a result. War is certainly without respect.

April 30, 1944.

Another Sunday is with us but military conditions are such that we are unable to hold any services. Jerry would give a lot to catch a congregation of men on the side of a mountain singing hymns. We do not intend to give him a chance. It is a grand day outside. I have been observing it from the inside of an old house that we expect at any moment will crawl away! I'm having the time of my life hunting down the fleas which take great delight in raising lumps over my poor old body. If we could only have a fire I would burn up all my clothes. There always seems to something to take the joy out of life.

The M.O. and I went on a house prowling expedition last night. I never had so much fun in a long time although we didn't find anything worthwhile. I guess the Hun, as he retreats, takes everything with him.

May 1, 1944.

It was quiet on the front tonight so I gathered a group of the lads behind a great rock and held a short service. Somehow religion has an appeal when we are under the nose of the Hun. While out there I had a couple of interviews with men who had just received news that their wives weren't playing the game. One poor lad broke down while he told me his story. I thought that Jerry would hear his sobs. I do wish we could do something to prevent such heartbreak in lives. I'm afraid there is going to be an awful mess in some of our Canadian homes when this business is over.

Part way back I was told that a few of our lads had been wounded and were on their way in. We organized a few extra stretcher bearers and went out to meet them. It's awfully tough getting our lads back in this area. Some of them ride the stretcher for two and three hours. They are certainly a brave lot. Fortunately none were fatally wounded but will be out of action for a long time.

May 2, 1944.

This is the sort of day I should be spending at a lovely Ontario lake. It is very hot and I have been sitting behind a stone barracade with only my shorts on having a sun bath. I managed to get a good sponge bath that was a bit over-due. I should now be free of fleas for a few days.

We had another good night. Just one casualty but not serious. Still, I'm a bit tired of seeing our poor lads getting it. It's the side of army life I want to forget as quickly as possible.

From all accounts we hear they are just about ready for the big push. I'm guessing that it will come between the 16th and 21st of the month. Now that they have Mr. King in England it might be a good time to start. He could get a good ringside seat and since he happens to be an expert 'fence-sitter', he'd enjoy it. His government hasn't many friends among the troops.

Out of the Line Again

May 8, 1944.

We pulled out of the front line on Friday night and got to our new area early Sunday morning. It's great to be out. It was a long enough time and while we didn't suffer as many casualties as we did on other occasions, we still had enough. I don't think I can ever get used to seeing men being shot and wounded. I'm happy in a way, that it's removed from the eyes of loved ones. Their share is already a great burden.

Our new resting area is quite good ... by far the best we ever had. All around us are grand vegetable gardens and fruit trees. We were issued our summer drill and the way the weather has turned we can use it. We wear shorts and rolled shirts during the day and when night comes we have to get into slacks with just our hands and faces uncovered. The malaria precautions are strict and since this country is full of it we have to be careful. No one knows how long we are going to be here. I shouldn't wonder that the next move will tie in with action on all fronts.

May 10, 1944.

I'm a long way from my quarters tonight visiting lads in one of our convalescent hospitals. I haven't seen some of the lads since we were first in action. There are a number here, so I will be staying over so that I can have a good visit with them. The men are all in decent buildings and appear to be most content.

The day was hot and in an open jeep one gets plenty of sunshine. The drive along the coast road was perfect for there were many interesting things to see. One of the places I stopped on my way back was the house where Greta Garbo went into seclusion for four years. It didn't impress me much apart from the beautiful rose gardens around the house. I don't know how she ever lived in the house but I suppose when one wants to "be alone" one can live anywhere. The old Italian who showed me around the place said she wasn't as much alone as the world was led to believe!

May 13, 1944.

The days are extremely hot. It must be 100 in the shade and the perspiration is running off me like a well-kept stream. We haven't too much ambition. One doesn't need much over here. The local inhabitants are all very busy in their gardens and it's really funny to see the women doing it all while the men hang around the streets in the local towns. The poor women get the worst end of the bargain in this country.

We have a local woman who comes along each day for our laundry. She brings along the cutest little fellow, just about three years old. He has won the hearts of us all. Yesterday I gave him some candy and before he took it he put his arms around my neck and kissed me.

Today I have been busy with sports and getting my next-of-kin letters off. I just got word that one of my lads who I saw in hospital and who I liked very much, has died.

Back to the War

May 18, 1944.

Our rest is over and we are on the move again. The news that we have received back indicates our success is even more than we expected. To know that we are gradually pushing Jerry back in this kind of country gives us all plenty of heart. Rest at the moment is a bit difficult. You move from one place to another, stop and start digging in. It's really quite remarkable how comfortable a hole in the ground can be!

May 21, 1944.

Today is not like Sunday. We had a bit of a hectic night, so remained in our slit trenches where I managed to get a few hours sleep. The more stuff Jerry sends over the deeper we dig. We are like rabbits. One can't help but reflect upon how man can become totally depraved when you see him at war. I only hope that our statesmen will be equal to the task of preventing war. You see so much useless destruction it makes one stop and wonder. At one of the spots where we halted for a little while, a young woman and a little boy came out of a cave where they had been living for weeks. They were starving and their clothes were in pieces. It almost made me cry to look upon them. The Germans have made things very difficult for many of these people.

Everything seems to be going fairly well on the front. Every now and then I'm just lifted off the ground by our guns which are only a few yards away. We are moving pretty fast and from all accounts coming in we are moving in the right direction.

May 26, 1944.

We have been on the go night and day. Our lads are doing a splendid job pushing Jerry right out of the war. They have taken a good number of prisoners and they are a poor lot. I have tried to talk to many of them. Almost all are glad to be out of the war. The wounded ones come to the R.A.P. and get dressed. I have fixed up a few myself. All in all things are going at top speed and much better than we anticipated. The boys went right through the Hitler Line without a hitch. I sat on a part of it all night. Thank God our casualties have been light. I just pray that it holds out.

May 28, 1944.

Our lads have just finished some of the most aggressive fighting that has been done in this Italian campaign. They were wonderful and the C.O. was outstanding. I'm really proud of them. On the whole, casualties have not been high, particularly when you consider the miles that were covered in the first drive. It's Sunday but we are just having a few hours rest. A chance to get a shave and wash.

All around us is plenty of destruction. I really don't know how Italy will ever rebuild her towns and cities. I have seen many Germans and I can't say that they are very impressive. They appear to be fed up and glad to be out of it.

May 30, 1944.

The Canadians are certainly making a name for themselves and our Unit in particular. Sometimes it is difficult to know how men can stand so much. I fancy that steady advance has much to do with keeping them up. We set up the R.A.P. in a house about 3:00 a.m. Again it must have been owned by a well-to-do family. It's very modern and has many lovely gardens, something which I haven't seen before. There are all kinds of Italians around the place giving us a welcome and getting some food. At my right hand is a little lad very interested in what I'm writing. He's talking to me all the time but I don't get it.

May 31, 1944.

We are still forging ahead and each day brings us into new areas and closer to Rome. We are clipping along at about five miles a day. I stopped off last night to bury some of our lads. They were all killed by mines. The Hun has them buried all over the place. I do this after each battle and then I find my way back to the Unit. At the place where we stopped last night I found the Italians friendly. They took me in and fixed up a room and a bed where I had a very good sleep. This morning they had warm water ready so I took a bath and had a general clean up. The roads are very dusty so one gets extremely dirty. Shortly I'll be moving up ahead to where the lads are located.

June 2, 1944.

Yesterday we reached our objective. We covered a distance of thirty miles and you can understand how tired while at the same time how delighted we were. You had only to look on the faces of the Italians who greeted us with kisses and fruit to know how pleased they were to see us. The Germans treated them very badly, taking all their food and livestock. Our first job was to feed them out of our rations. As well there was a steady stream of men, women and children coming to the R.A.P. to get their wounds dressed. There was one little lad I fixed up who had a bad shrapnel wound in the head. He cried pretty hard but after I finished he wiped his dirty little face with his hands, smiled and thanked me.

I had to come back thirty miles to get all my burials looked after. It's an awful business. On the whole our casualties were not high. High enough, however, to cause a lot of sorrow back home in Canada. We look as if we have the Hun on the run here. Perhaps we'll get a bit of a rest.

June 3, 1944.

We are still enjoying our rest but there are many who just want to keep going now that we have the Hun on the move. Of course we will get our share again so they need not hurry too much. Rome is getting closer and closer and I have an idea that when it goes, the Hun will be pretty well cleaned up in this country. The days are extremely hot and just leaves one helpless. The nights, however, are quite cool and that helps to put you right away when you do get to bed.

I'm getting tanned up like a real Italian, but is my hair ever getting grey. I had it cut this morning and so help me I thought the barber was cutting my grandfather's hair!

The papers will soon be reporting our officer casualties. I can't mention them except to say that none of them is serious. Our officers did well during the advance. The C.O. also excelled and I'll be greatly disappointed if he doesn't get a D.S.O. out of it.

June 4, 1944.

This morning I held a memorial service for all the lads who had fallen since we started our campaign. The C.O. read the names out and then we had a memorial prayer, followed by the Last Post and Reveille ... the pipe band and bugler doing the honours in fine fashion. Our total dead number 56. It is not too high they say for the work done, but to me just one is too many.

We are still having a rest. The boys look remarkably well after their big drive. I trust for their sakes they won't have to go in again too soon. This morning it was announced that the Yanks were in Rome and we are trying to find out all the details.

I came south this morning to visit the hospitals and I drove over what has been the battlefield for the past few weeks. You can hardly imagine the destruction. There is just nothing left of Cassino Monastery and the surrounding hills. It's fine to know that we are marching forward. I pray that we will be successful on all fronts and end this business.

June 8, 1944.

I just got in last night after a 300 mile trip covering all of our hospitals. I managed to see all my lads, who despite their wounds were in the very best of spirits. We are still in the resting area and there is no word on when we move off again. The news coming in from the west is good. It took us a long time to get going but we sure hit hard when we did. The fall of Paris will do more harm to German morale than anything so far. The weather here is still extremely warm, but after the rotten winter we put in, I'm satisfied. Daily, I'm getting brown as a berry.

Yesterday we had the General in to see us and he gave the men a most inspiring talk. Although we are still at rest, I have been busy with next-of-kin letters. It's hard now that the aftermath of the battle is being felt. The letters for next-of-kin will be finished today. It's a big job and seems to take a lot out of me. I do feel so sorry for all the loves ones in Canada. It must be terrible when they get the tragic news.

June 15, 1944.

It is a fact that men write more regularly under battle conditions than they do at any other time. I have yet to find a man in our Unit who does not write home at least twice a week, except in those cases where there is some domestic trouble. My next-of-kin letters have been completed. It has taken me five days. One has to be so careful, for every word means so much to those dear ones who are called to sorrow at the passing of loved ones. You can't afford to be careless and since I write them all by hand it does take some time.

Yesterday I visited the graves of the lads to make sure in battle quickness I had not overlooked any detail. I found everything in order. At noon we stopped at an Italian farm house to prepare for a bite to eat. We pulled in behind the house to get some shade, for it was very hot. There we came upon the family mixing up cement to start their rebuilding job. They were glad to see us and while Ted was making the tea I noticed one of the girls had put a bad gash in her shin with the shovel. I got out my first-aid kit and called her over to fix it up. In about ten minutes men, women and children (I don't know where they came from) were on hand to have the "Canadian doctor" fix up their scars. The pay off came when an old fellow who could speak a little English, asked me to visit his daughter who was in bed about to have a baby. I had to tell him that I was in a big hurry and by then I really was! My supplies were running low and my temperature high! They were grateful for what I did and gave me some eggs. I reached the Unit around six, had supper, a sponge bath and went off to bed.

Last night I heard that the Tely reported that I was wounded. I wish they hadn't mentioned anything about me. My nick was so trivial I didn't see any reason to tell anyone.

June 17, 1944.

Except for meals, I have sat around sheltering myself from a most devastating rain storm. I was awakened early this morning by rumbling thunder the likes of which I have never heard before. I thought I was back in the front lines.

The spot where we are is rather pleasant to the eye and ear. From where I am located, I look down into a fertile valley. At the top is the usual olive trees in strict formation. In between their cultivated rows are the plum, cherry and apple trees. On the plain and running up the slope of the mountains, on the other side, are square patches of grain fields ever so golden and in the process of being harvested.

There are all kinds of small farm houses scattered irregularly over the landscape. These are the homes of the peasants who work the land for the 'Padrone.'

It has been a good change. The noise and toil of battle is not pleasant. Living like an animal is unacceptable and seeing men who had scarcely begun their voyage, cut off, broken in body and mind, is sometimes more than I can understand. When you are in the thick of it, it sometimes doesn't enter your thoughts. It's only when you get away from it all and have time for reflection that it hurts the most. When this business is over we must keep it so much alive in our world that it can never happen again. In the coming days of peace I will be at the forefront in renouncing warlords and dictators who crush the manhood and womahood of our nations.

I'm Off to the South on Leave

June 20, 1944.

I was away from early morning to very late last night looking for a lad in detention. I think I covered all of southern Italy in my search. About 5:00 p.m., after 100 miles of searching I found the lad and had a good chat with him. I have been working on his case for sometime and I feel I'm going to be rewarded for my efforts. His poor mother is greatly worried so I hope I can write her soon and tell her that I have him back with the Unit.

At the moment Ted is packing my kit as I'm going down to the south for a seven day leave. The M.O. and Captain Fisher the paymaster, make up our party. The weather here has now cleared up and should make for a pleasant leave. The fact that we are being granted leaves indicates that we are not going into action for at least a little while.

I read an article by Churchill yesterday in which he stated, "If our plans workout the enemy should be defeated this summer." That's the first time I can remember him being so definite and optimistic. Everything is going Very well and I shouldn't wonder if the Hun won't be looking for a way out pretty soon. We can't be too easy on him. The old story of not kicking a dog when he is down should not be part of our thinking. We must keep the German in check or we will have a repetition of war in another twenty years. This must be the war to end wars.

June 22, 1944.

We got into our rest area around 5:30 p.m. The first thing that we had to do was to report to the office, where we signed a book, were given the details of the camp and finally issued with writing paper, smokes and a couple of chocolate bars. Then we were cleared and an efficient English sergeant, in broken Italian, spoke to a lad who was all dressed up in a white suit. The lad quickly took us to our tent which is exactly 100 yards from the water and there he unpacked the trunk and put the tent in order. Our M.r. who speaks Italian went to work on him and in no time at all the things we forgot to bring were placed neatly under our beds (washbasin, fly nets etc.). The floor of our tent is concrete, covered with a kind of rough mat. In each corner are four spring beds, made up with white sheets which will be well used, believe me.

After we had a shower and changed into our evening dress (slacks and shirts) we came over to the mess for supper. The supper was exceptional, in fact I had two helpings of dessert (apple pie and cheese). After supper we went to a stage show 'Double Scotch' which as the name suggests, had an all Scottish cast. It was full of good clean humour and the talent was tops.

This morning we didn't get up until 8:00 a.m. I had a quick wash and came over to a very appetizing breakfast. When we finished we returned to our tent where our Italian batman was busy cleaning and fixing up our shoes and clothes. Fortunately for us he also happens to be a barber, so reclining in a most comfortable position on my bed, I had a grand shave. He tells me that he will give me one each morning. All of us jumped into our bathing suits and finished the morning in the warm blue waters of the Mediterranean. It's a great way to build an appetite for dinner which again proved most satisfying.

June 23, 1944.

Darkness is just descending over our very peaceful camp. It is very difficult to believe that there is a war going on. I'm sitting in a well constructed, elaborately furnished lounge. The radio is bringing in some good music. The rest camp is very cosmopolitan. It should be called the 'Unit d'Nations Rest Camp'. There are officers from all over the world. Everyone is congenial and that helps the spirit of our surroundings. The camp stretches for miles along the shores of the Mediterranean and there is no end to the things you can see and do. There are sports fields for every taste; club rooms for men who like Indoor games. There are two very fine show complexes ... one for stage and the other for movies. They are on the go each evening. The library has a good selection of books. I'm reading the 'Minstrel in France' by Harry Lauder. It's dedicated to his only son whom he lost in France in 1917. Our meal schedule is just what the doctor ordered. Around eight, our Italian batman brings us a cup of tea in bed. Whoever finishes first gets the first shave. Breakfast comes at nine, dinner at one, afternoon tea at four, supper at seven.

This morning we drove into Salerno and gave the city a good going over. We returned in time for afternoon tea and then headed for a swim. While I was out in the water I heard a voice from the shore. It was one of our officers who was calling me in. When I arrived on shore the lad handed me a letter from the C.O. He wants me to take the Unit up to Rome and thus to return immediately. I'll be off in the morning for our Unit and then on to Rome.

It's a Hospital Bed For Me

July 7, 1944.

I have been in hospital this past week with some kind of new pneumonia. The doctor was telling me that it's something new they are running into and so far know very little about. I was on the second day at the rest camp when the thing struck me. The M.O. thought I was getting malaria so advised me to go down to see the camp M.O. He took my temperature and it was 103, so he packed me off fast to the hospital.

My first few days were the worst. I couldn't eat or sleep and generally speaking was a bit hard to handle. I got plenty of good attention and although I'm very weak, I'm feeling brighter and sense that the fever is passing. So far I have no idea how long I'm to be here.

July 8, 1944.

I'm feeling very much better today. I washed myself this morning and that's a sure indication I'm on my way to recovery. I had a letter from Toronto telling me that one of the "hide-behind-the-pulpit" young ministers had said we padres were on a picnic. It so happened that I had a very difficult night, climbed four miles of mountain and was shot at while out burying a lad. When I got in I was cut, wet and bruised. When I read this letter and saw its contents, I wrote one stinging reply. Among other things, I said that I was damn fed up with the attitude of some of our Presbyterian ministers. I have no doubt that I will repeat my same thoughts when I return home ... this time on a more personal level.

July 9, 1944.

It's early Sunday morning and I just had my bed made. Since I'm washed and readied I'm prepared for the day. I'm expecting Ted down to see me some time today. I'm feeling much better with each day. One of these mornings I should be up and walking around.

I just remembered a funny story that happened to me while in Rome. I was resting in my hotel room when Lloyd Saunders, our dental officer, came rushing in and said "Dave, I was just stopped downstairs by an Irishwoman from Cork, who wants to meet a real living Irishman." He took me with him and we found her living in a nice apartment. When we stepped in Lloyd introduced me as the Chaplain of the Irish. "So your from Dublin and a Chaplain of the Irish," she said, "Now, Father, I'm so pleased to meet you." She grasped me around the neck with both hands, kissed my Irish ring and did a real bow! I was just about to tell her that I was a Protestant when in came two more women. 'Meet Father Rowland." "God bless you, Father, and may the saints preserve you," were their first words. They went on to ask me all kinds of questions while Saunders, sitting in the corner having a good laugh, wasn't any help at all. "You will have to meet Father Flasker," they said, "He will give you some Holy Water to take home." Still I waited for the opportunity to tell them the whole story, when more people came In. I was just looking for an excuse to go when the woman began arranging for a private confession in her home, to which they all were to come that evening. Ain't it funny some of the things that happen to you! Saunders and I had a real laugh as we drove back to the hotel.

I'm feeling stronger each day and shouldn't wonder after the M.O. had told me that he will permit me to get up. Ted was in and says that there is still no sign of a move for us. We are being kept out quite a long while. It's difficult to imagine what they will do with us next. I can't see us doing much more fighting in this country. We have almost achieved all we can here. Maybe they will send us to the Balkans or to France.

July 11, 1944.

This is my eleventh day in bed. The doctor promises to let me up tomorrow. The routine here is pretty severe. You are awakened at 6:00 a.m. and are kept awake by the nurses taking temperatures and giving you pills. The lights are put out at 10:00 p.m. so you must go off to sleep. The meals are excellent. It seems that they believe in feeding you well in the British hospitals.

A large number of the nursing sisters in the wards come from Ireland. Naturally making known my nationality has paid a few extra dividends in food and tea. The C.O. and George Duncan came in to see me this afternoon. The C.O. just returned from a leave in Cairo. He says you need lots of money there, for it is most expensive. As usual he told me not to hurry and take a lot of rest. There is no sign of our Unit moving so he added "a good long rest." As always he is tops with me.

July 13, 1944.

Yesterday Ted and my educational corporal came to see me. The corporal told me he had been doing some letter writing for me. They brought me lots of mail. I had letters from wives and mothers of men killed in action. They are most appreciative for the things that have been done, but my they are hard to read, particularly where there are little children involved. War is truly a terrible thing.

Today I sat up for the first time for about four hours. I'm hoping when the M.O. does his rounds that he will permit me to put on my clothes. The news we get daily is most encouraging. Russia will soon be on German soil. They are only 30 miles from East Prussia. There should be a fine reaction to Hitler's oft repeated statement, "Never a foreign soldier will set foot on German soil." The battle in France is making slow but steady progress. I expected the French to contribute more than they seem to have to assist the cause. I'm afraid they may set their sails to the wind.

July 15, 1944.

I still haven't managed to get into my clothes. I seem to be taking an extra long time. I get up around noon and sit in a chair till about four and then back to bed. I must say that I'm feeling pretty good but lack pep and ambition. I have an English major in the next bed to me. He calls me 'Canada' all the time and when speaking about Canadians says 'bloody good show, Canada.' He found a flea in his bed yesterday and so help me you would have thought he was out after a German patrol the way he went after it. He's always good for a laugh and that's something in hospital. I'm worried that the Unit will move while I'm laid up and it might be difficult to catch up. While I'm not overly anxious to see any more fighting, if the Unit moves into action I would want to be there with them.

This is not a very exciting life. Patients come and go. Except for the major beside me, I'm the oldest patient in the ward. One of the pleasant things here is the news that we get. We listen to it about six times a day. Things here are not moving all that quickly, except for the Russians who will be in East Prussia and that should add to the growing headaches of poor old Hitler and his gang. I sometimes think that they will be ready for unconditional surrender rather than have us fight on German soil.

Convalescence on the Mediterranean

July 20, 1944.

Yesterday I was discharged from hospital and sent by ambulance to the convalescent home. The ride got me down a bit. I was well treated in the British hospital and can speak most highly of their medical care and personal attention.

The convalescent home is quite attractive and spacious. It's ideally located, situated right on the shores of the blue Mediterranean. The food is of the highest order and liberally served. My room is a charming spot and I have an outstanding view over the water where sailboats seem to play the day long.

I was able to see the M.O. this morning and he assures me that in a couple of weeks I'll be fine. I still can't figure out how I got pneumonia in the first place. I was feeling so well even though our time in the line was a bit severe. Guess it's just one of those things. So far the Unit is out of the line and the only thing we are hearing are rumours. We are having a long period of rest. Soon, I feel, it will be over and we will be on the move again.

I heard on the radio that an attempt was made on Hitler's life. Rather too bad they didn't manage to "bump" him off. This incident may indicate internal conditions in Germany. Getting Leghorn and Ancona will make a big difference in the fighting here.

July 23, 1944.

Here it is another Sunday. I've been out of harness so long that I'll have to learn all over again. It's a grand morning over here. At the moment the nearby park is crowded with children having the time of their lives. I have noticed that you never see children playing with skipping ropes, balls or any kind of toys. So far I've never seen any Italian children playing any sort of games.

Bill Reid and I went down to see an Italian musical last night. It wasn't too bad even though we didn't understand what it was all about. The music was good and they played a good selection of Well-known American pieces. There was one girl with a wonderful voice and I suppose to make a hit with all the soldiers present, sang three songs in English. The audience is rather amusing. They shout and talk to the people on the stage and now and then you get a conversation between stage and audience.

John Humphries was in to see me last night. He was saying that there was still no sign of a move for us. Of course, so many things happen so quickly these days I pay little attention to the obvious.

I feel that I should be back with the Unit although I know that they can manage very well without me. I'm nearly a month away but since they are doing nothing but sitting around, I haven't missed anything. I still can't understand why we have been kept out of the line so long. It's going to be tough to get back into the swing of things again.

I have fallen in love with me bed! It's grand to sleep between sheets and actually wash and shower from a basin. There is another Canadian padre in now by the name of Stew East. We spend a lot of time together.

July 27, 1944.

It's four years today since I received my commission in the army. If they keep me around much longer they will be sending me out on the 'over-age' policy. It won't be long until they will be discharging us. Everyday Germany is getting closer to defeat. It would be mighty interesting to know what is actually happening inside Germany these days. If only unrest and dissension would start in the army it would hasten the end. So far the German soldier is fighting pretty fiercely.

Last night Stew East and I went off to the show, but again it was on the rocks. The sound was so terrible you just couldn't hear a thing. We got disgusted and left.

There is still no sign of a move. The Unit is just doing some routine training. We seem to be getting a very good break. It would be great to think that the fighting is over. It bothers me greatly to think of the poor lads who will suffer so much going through another attack.

I must be feeling better today. I have asked for seconds with every meal. I think the Italian waiters are thoroughly disgusted wlth me.

July 28, 1944.

I'm afraid if they keep me here much longer, I won't be fit to return to the Unit. The hotel atmosphere with all its comforts is making me lazy. This morning Stew and I were driven for a ride along the coast. We stopped at a huge villa that had been visited on a number of occasions by Mussolini. One of his big shots lived in this spot. It is now a convalescent home. We had tea and were shown around the place. The owner was a shipbuilder, so has the villa designed in accordance with the layout of a ship. It was very novel. From here we had a perfect view of Capri which is only six miles away. By the way I won't be visiting Capri. The outrageous prices the Italians want to charge you to take you over doesn't wash. I won't be a sucker!

August 2, 1944.

I learned from Ted that the King gave the Unit a pretty good inspection. I was sorry to have missed it.

According to the radio today Germany has received yet another set-back. Turkey has broken off diplomatic and political relations. Had she declared war it would have been another headache for Hitler. All in all the dark shades of defeat are gradually enveloping Germany, while the sun of victory is getting warmer each day for us.

My daily routine still consists of writing, reading, boating and swimming. Sometimes I take a walk up the streets of Sorrento, but it smells to high heaven in spots, so it doesn't take much to drive me back home. My days here are nearly over. I'm very pleased that the C.O. has kept my spot vacant, for as is the general rule, just as soon as any rank, whether through sickness or any other cause, leaves, his place is immediately filled. The reason of course, is that the Regiment must always be up to strength in the field. The fact that the Regiment was not in action helped a bit. Had they been in battle they would need a padre. Since I'm one of the few padres in the Canadian Army that has managed to remain with his Regiment from the beginning, I would want to finish up with the Irish.

Yesterday was a big day for us on the front. The crack is getting bigger each day. Looks too, like Hitler is really having a bit of trouble on the home front. Present conditions look bright and we can only pray that the end will come before more lives are lost.

August 6, 1944.

When Sundays come I always feel I should be doing a little preaching. I have forgotten how long it has been since I conducted a service.

Yesterday Stew East and I took a tour of Sorrento. At one store where we went in to look around, I found in my conversation with one of the ladies that ran it, that they sold most of their inlaid wares to the T. Eaton Co. I guess it's a pretty small world after all. She showed me an excellent coffee table all inlaid with colored designs. It was priced around $200.00. Had I anyway of getting it home I would have bought it. It certainly wouldn't fit into a soldier's parcel!

This will be my last day at the convalescent home. I wonder how I'm going to go back to roughing it. The contrast between sleeping in a bed and a truck is going to be a large one.

At Last I'm Back with the Regiment

August 13, 1944.

No sooner had I arrived back with the Unit than we were sent on a scheme. When we returned I headed down the road to the mobile baths and spent a good long time under a cold shower.

Things are extremely quiet. Were it not for the many rumours going around, I wouldn't know what too expect next. The only rumour I'm interested in is when the end will come. Daily the news becomes more hopeful. The progress in France is more than anyone expected. If they managed to cut off the German 10th Army as reported it would be easy going to Paris. Florence has fallen and that gives us more scope to move in this mountainous country.

One feature in the Unit these days is the betting on the month the war will end. It's interesting to note that no one goes beyond December and most centre around October.

August 16, 1944.

The good news today was the successful landing in the south of France. The fact the opposition so far has been light may indicate how hard pressed Hitler is to keep all parts of his fronts reinforced. The landing will help us here, as it will cut off another road of supply to his army in Italy.

I'm now back in the groove again. I spent yesterday visiting the lads in the hospitals and had a few men to see me with domestic problems. I'll be so happy when I'm released from such sad things. Today was one of my typical chaplain days. It started with six personal interviews, all domestic. I got in a couple of 'Padre's Hours' and finished the evening by attending an excellent concert in our own lines, put on by a visiting Canadian party.

August 21, 1944.

It now looks like the Germans can do little to stop the drive in France and are headed for the Fatherland as quickly as they can. With the fall of Paris imminent, it will give a lot of encouragement to our men. On the other hand it should have a disasterous effect on German morale at home and in the front lines.

These are very hot days in Italy. It must be 100 in the shade from about 9:00 a.m. to 4:00 P.m. The fleas and mosquitoes are here in the millions. You can't take a meal without them wanting a large share of it. During our sleeping hours we have to use nets and rub on a repellent which seems to work pretty well. Unfortunately there is quite a lot of malaria around. The lads who seem to contact it are over it in about seven days.

It is most encouraging to hear Monty make the statement, *'The end is now in sight.'* His judgment in the past has been very sound. I'm sure he wouldn't make a statement to his troops unless he was sure of himself.

August 29, 1944.

Sunday afternoon I had a service with the lads and it was so hot we all had to sit down under a tree to get a bit of shade. Sunday night I contacted Smith. We had a good chat and I'm afraid if our fellow clergyman heard us they would have been a little disgusted. We are getting a little browned-off to say the least.

We were also discussing what we would do with the grants the government is going to give us after the war. I think my benefit will work out to about $1800.00 It all sounds pretty good from this distance and it is amusing to hear the lads suggest what they are going to do with it. For some reason or other, chicken farming seems to be the plan that gets the most votes. Maybe it's because we have seen so few eggs and chickens in our army life.

For the allies this has been an outstanding month of military successes. By the time we reach the end of September I would be surprised if we are not close to the end of the war with Germany. The news in the morning indicated more trouble in the Balkans. They will soon follow in the footsteps of Rumania. We are making pretty steady progress here. As soon as we can get the enemy out of the hills and unto the Plains of Lombardy, he will pretty well have had it in this country. The lads have had a real difficult time in these mountains and I shouldn't be surprised if they will all want to migrate to B.C. to feel at home.

September 5, 1944.

I'm far away from my truck but found this Hun paper to write on. Things are going along pretty well with us. We are now pushing him back hourly. I'm travelling with the R.A.P. and must say that the M.O. likes to get up close where he can do the most good. I think our Unit M.O. is doing an excellent job in this war. Naturally fighting every day and night doesn't give much time for eating or sleeping. We are hoping when we get him out on the plains, which we can see at a distance, we will get a few days rest.

September 12, 1944.

We are out of the line for a few hours rest. I had a wonderful sleep last night. It's really a treat to break away from the noise of battle. I have a full day ahead of me so I intend to get started on the next-of-kin letters. We have gone through our hardest and cruelest fighting. The Irish captured the town of Coriano and it was another Cassino. The Hun tried his best with everything he had to hold it, but our lads proved just a little better and it was soon in our hands. Our M.O. was wounded but not seriously. Jerry blew our R.A.P. in on us while we were attending the wounded. I can't figure out why the Hun wants to hang on here, however, we are pushing him back.

September 17, 1944.

I had a very busy morning. I held a memorial service for our fallen lads. The service was attended by our General, the Brigadier and many other military '*brass hats.*' When I got back from conducting another service for one of the other units, the Colonel sent for me and when I saw him he told me the General had asked him to convey personally to me, his appreciation for the service. I had taken for my text: '*Greater love hath no man than this that a man lay down his life for his friends.*'

After dinner I'm making a trip to the hospitals. I will be away for a few days ... I have many men to see. I pray that we are over the worst of the fighting. I never again want the lads to go through what they have just finished. I'm awfully proud of the Irish, for I feel in the past few weeks they have written a most colourful chapter in the history of our Canadian fighting men. I'm only sad that so many were wounded and so many of our fine lads paid with their lives. The sorrow created in our Canadian homes must be tremendous. I pray that God will comfort the mothers and wives.

Let's Not Forget the Wounded

September 18, 1944.

I got away with Bill Elder right after dinner yesterday to start a hospital visitation. We got several hospitals visited in the afternoon. We stopped at the coastal town of Fano for the night. We found a very good house, where our batman set up our beds and made us most comfortable. The first thing we did this morning was get out of bed right into the Adriatic for a morning swim. That was at 7:00 a.m. Not bad for a couple of veterans.

We headed south for our next hospital, where we found about a dozen of our men. All were feeling well, although some were very badly wounded. We had a wonderful dinner at the hospital officers! mess. Elder said that he felt like going back for more. After dinner we pushed south and hoped to make Perugia before dark, but the roads were so packed with convoys that we made very poor time. Darkness was well upon us when we were within 20 miles of our objective. We just pulled over to the side of the road and had our supper in a Carbinieri barracks. The Italian soldiers got quite a kick out of us. After we shared our smokes with them, there wasn't anything they wouldn't do for us. They found us an excellent place to sleep.

Since we are a good many miles from the front, everything is most peaceful and calm. I see lights showing from the windows throughout the little town. Jerry just doesn't come this far back.

I woke up and turned on the 7:00 a.m. news. The outlook gets better all the time. They didn't say anything about our front, although when we left we were only about three miles from Rimini. Once that is taken we are out on the plains and things should go a lot faster.

September 21, 1944.

I'm getting to see a good number of my lads. To date I have seen 118. I hope to get finished by tonight or early in the morning. I'm now at my eighth hospital with two more to go. The lads are thrilled to see someone from the Unit.

I don't know what the Unit is doing. They were out for a couple of days when I left on Sunday and I only pray they don't have to go in again for a while. This had been the busiest time in all of our battles. I pray that the whole rotten business will soon be over.

The news continues to be good. I still can't figure out why Jerry wants to hang on when he knows he's licked. Why he wants to put up the fight that he continues around Rimini is beyond me. I guess Jerry wants to see Italy destroyed before he leaves it.

September 23, 1944.

It's only been a couple of hours since I arrived back at the Unit. I was away six days. In that time I visited ten hospitals and covered 800 miles. I managed to see 130 men. I'm pleased to report that of all the wounded I visited, only one may not make it.

The war news continues to be good. The fact that Rimini has fallen should make the going a bit better for us. We will be pursuing Jerry on the plains and that will be an advantage for us. I will never forget the 'hills of Italy' in fact, I'm not sure that I will ever want to see a hill or mountain again.

The R.A.P. is located in a very dirty Italian house a few miles from the front line. The fleas give me a real going over. I will get around to all the companies and give them a report on my hospital visitations. In all likelihood, Jerry will interrupt my sojourns with his shelling.

We Are on the Plains of Lombardy

September 26, 1944.

At long last we are on the Lombardy Plains. I was never more thankful when I drove down my last Italian hill, just as it was getting dark last night. The countryside is now covered with olive and orange orchards and looks quite pretty.

Last night it rained quite hard so we are ploughing through a lot of mud this morning. We managed to find a house for our R.A.P., so missed having to be out in it. It was quite comfortable where the M.O. and I slept until we were heavily attacked by a battalion of bed-bugs. I sat up half the night trying to get rid of them. Some managed to get through my defence so I'm well covered with their trade marks this morning.

The daily news continues to be good. From the French side they're surely closing right in on Germany. As for the Balkans, Hitler just hasn't any support there at all. While the going is very slow here, we are managing to push him back. If the weather holds out our tanks should make good progress on the plains.

All around us this morning the Italians are returning. You should see them when they look on what once was their homes. There are a couple of old women around right now and they are crying hysterically. Apparently the Hun not only mined their homes but killed part of their family. It is a most tragic sight.

September 28, 1944.

We are still doing our stuff. It's a busy job and keeps one on the move night and day. I would just love to find a spot where peace and calm would allow me a chance to write. While we are making excellent progress, I'm a bit tired of this whole business. War and its physical pain and constant hardships is something no one can ever get accustomed to. What I have seen has made me come to the conclusion that I will dedicate the rest of my life to preaching against it. Thank God that none of our families have had to suffer the material destruction or lamentable suffering which is so evident among the men, women and children of this country. All day yesterday they came in flocks to have their wounds dressed. I feel so sorry for the defenceless children.

The grind is pretty steady and unfortunately the chaplain with the M.O. are the only two who can't get a day or two off in battle. The weather is turning wet and cold. I only hope we can get through here before the winter sets in.

September 29, 1944.

The weather is still horrible and reminds me of the days we spent in the hills last winter. Of course we have the shelter of a house and that makes our position a little better than the poor lads who have to live their days and nights in slit trenches. Would to God that victory and peace would come quickly!

We have a fine moonlight night but those of us who live under its peaceful shades are anything but calm. The night just vibrates with the sound and the destruction of war. The old house where I'm located just shakes off a coat of dust, brick and mortar everytime a shell lands anywhere near it.

September 30, 1944.

FOr the first time in about a week we have had a beautiful sunny day, thus drying up some of this awful mud that has been slowing down our progress and spoiling some of our plans. So far being on the plains has not increased our speed. We have to fight very hard for every bit of ground gained. When one takes a look at the many prisoners coming in one can't see anything superior in their appearance (which seems to indicate that they can't hold us up much longer). I noticed a good number of very young boys, perhaps 17 or 18, were captured today. They hadn't even started shaving. They did a little job for me and then I sent them on. One of them, who could speak a little English, (after I had given him a little food) said that it was the first food he had to eat in three days.

I had a little work to do today that left my spirits a little low. A lot of the things I see daily are very hard to do and difficult to understand.

October 2, 1944.

From the point of view of casualties this was a perfect day. The kind of a day that everyone is glad to see and no one more so than the M.O. and myself. We have certainly had our share. I can only hope and pray that from the sacrifice of our young men will come a world of everlasting peace. To give so very much and not attain it, would be a shame and disgrace upon our civilization. I pray that when victory comes, we will be as diligent in our preparations for peace as we have been for war. I never want to see our children going through what our lads are going through this very hour.

This has been a very miserable day. It hasn't stopped raining since early morning. I went out to bury one of the lads and as I laid him away I began to think that even the elements were waging war on me. I was drenched to the skin and had to have a complete change of clothes when I got back to the R.A.P.

We are certainly disappointed to have been held up by the mud. We expected to be across the plains, had it remained dry. Now I'm afraid we will suffer several weeks delay. War cares not for personal desires and human affairs ... of course there are many bright spots in the other fronts.

Colonel Ralston is visiting us at the moment. I'm afraid he is not getting a very good reception from the Canadian troops. There is much wrong in our set-up and the lads are going to make it known to him.

October 3, 1944.

Today it has stopped raining and I pray it will stay that way so we can get going again. Jerry is holding a bit of ground I'm very, very anxious to get into, as I know we have a few casualties there. It's much better to be able to inform the people back home of some definite news about their loved ones. '*Missing*' or '*suspected prisoner of war*', is not very consoling. I trust that the missing we have, turn out to be captured. Last night I had an excellent sleep in our cow shed. It was so good that I even had time to do some worthwhile dreaming.

I see that the Telegram is writing up on the Irish. Some of the lads deserve all they can say and write about them. The M.O. is coming along all right and should be back with us in a couple of weeks. We were all very lucky the morning he got hit. It's part of the game and you can't worry much about it.

October 6, 1944.

Old man weather is still playing on the side of the Jerry. I thought it was going to clear up yesterday, but this morning it is raining buckets. It is now estimated that the weather has set our operation back one whole month. I'm still hopeful that the success attained on other fronts will eventually effect us here and thus relieve the pressure. While we are now making progress we are not having casualties. No matter how black a picture there is always a ray of light to give a little hope. In war you just have to take the good with the bad.

When we arrived at our farmyard, it was pretty well stocked with cattle, pigs and chickens. Today I was wandering around a bit and I find a complete absence of the dear little things. Of course there has been a bit of shelling and I'm sure it has conveniently put some of the animals right on our dinner plates!

October 7, 1944.

Today hasn't been too pleasant and right now we are having a pretty hot time. On several occasions I have had some nasty interruptions. It's amazing though, how you accustom yourself to some of the strange things you have to do in an awful hurry. Often I think I'll be startled more than once by a car backfiring, and I'll be wanting to run for cover. There are times when I feel very little mercy for those who have caused this business. It's terrible how one loses faith in humanity. I suppose though (and I notice it when I have to handle some prisoners) you quickly recover your faith in the proper principles of justice. I only hope our prisoners of war receive the same good treatment we give the Germans. We heard today that a landing had been made on the Greek mainland. It's nice to have a bit of sunshine somewhere.

October 12, 1944.

Tonight I'm a good bit away from the front line. We were relieved the evening of the 10th and managed to get out without any casualties. Since the M.O. and I were the last to leave we had to move off on our own, hoping to find the Unit. We weren't successful, so managed to find a comfortable hotel and went off to sleep. Next morning we got up about ten and went down to the coffee shop, got what we could and headed off to find the Unit. It didn't take us long to locate the men since they were just a mile away. On our arrival we learned that a search party had been looking for us. The c.o. thought that we might have run into some trouble on coming out of the line. I really think he believed that we were taken prisoner. Not me!

Today I was doing a new job. A week ago as I hinted, 'A' company was cut off and taken prisoner. I have been waiting for Jerry to pull out of the area so I could get in and look around. I made it this morning. I found five dead lads and it now looks as though the rest have taken a ride with Jerry. I came upon most of their equipment which indicated they were told to strip it off and get going. Since there were a good many mines in the area, I didn't like to take any chances. I'm going back tomorrow to have a further look.

October 13, 1944.

We had a lovely day today and the sun shone as it hasn't done for many the long day. As a result things are again moving on the front. We are now getting fixed up in our area. At the moment I'm living in quite a decent house. I have George Duncan as my roommate and that makes things most agreeable. The house is pretty well up to date and furnished in a modern fashion. Our lights and water are cut-off most of the time, since most of the installations have been bombed out. I learned that in peace time this Adriatic town of Riccioni was patronized by English, French and American tourists. Possibly that explains the modern decor. A couple of weeks here should help our morale. We had an extra long time in the line and I can tell you we are all a pretty tired lot.

Today I went back to the area where 'A' company was captured. I found several bodies that had been buried by Italians. In order to identify them we had to dig them up. Most of the party was sick. The only thing that kept me going was my fear that if I got sick, the rest might give up the job. I only pray that I never again have to do a job like that, although for the loved ones at home, it is the only way to set their minds at rest. I think it far better to know one way or the other.

October 17, 1944.

All I have done for the past 48 hours is put words to paper. Nothing new or startling is happening here these days. The lads are having a good rest, seeing lots of shows and managing to get in a few pleasure trips to places of interest. The private in this man's army doesn't do too badly.

I'm hoping to get off this week to visit the hospitals. Of course, if we are to go back into the line after our two weeks are up, I won't get very far. It is most important to me that we look after the personal needs of our wounded and sick men.

I'm still pretty convinced that 'A' company has been taken prisoner. Jerry may have taken some of our wounded back with him, but the fact that one wounded man who could not walk, was left, leads me to believe that those who were taken are all right. I hope that the Red Cross will soon get some word to the anxious loved ones.

October 18, 1944.

According to the entry I made in my diary a year ago, the war was suppose to be over today! Guess I'm not a very good prophet. Still with all the pounding that Germany has taken of late, it is surprising that she hasn't thrown in the towel. The authorities over here have us pretty well convinced that we will be another winter in Italy. The weather has been so bad I'm sure it has set us back a few months. I'm still hopeful that we won't have to stay here. I would welcome a change to another front in preference to another Italian winter. The Regiment is still out of the line. There has been a lot going on for the lads but so far I have been tied down to letter writing. I will be finished tonight, so tomorrow I hope to pack up and go off for a couple of days rest. I would like to go down to Rome, but the distance is great and you can't get much of a rest if you spend most of the time driving over the Italian roads.

October 22, 1944.

I started out on Friday morning to make my rounds of the hospitals and have been on the go most of the time. I got as far as Fabiano Friday night, where I was invited to stay with a section of South Africans. They treated me royally and had I been a drinking man I shouldn't wonder but I would be there yet! I got to Perugia yesterday afternoon and by the time I had completed my visitation it was getting close to midnight.

This morning I'm heading back home. It's a long trip and since the roads are packed with convoys it takes hours to make a few miles. All the men I visited were in pretty good shape. Unfortunately some are badly wounded so will be heading back to Canada.

Things appear to be quiet on all fronts.

October 23, 1944.

It was quite late by the time I got back to the Unit last night. We drove steadily most of the day but the convoys on the road held us up. I managed to get to three of our hospitals this time. I saw 50 men. They were all remarkably well ... all agree that it's a grand experience sleeping between sheets and having regular meals. A number of them will be going home and despite their wounds are quite happy at the prospect.

When I arrived last night I learned that the lads had gone into the line again. I was so tired that I just stayed behind and will follow them in the morning. It will be a couple of days before they bump into the enemy so I will be there in plenty of time.

October 25, 1944.

I'm back in the line again. I spent a good part of the day yesterday trying to catch up with the troops. So far this has been our quietest front line experience. We are hoping that we have come to a place in the campaign where Jerry is pulling out. We haven't made contact with him for a couple of days. He has left many mines and unfortunately these have caused some serious casualties.

At the moment I'm sitting in my truck while a party is digging a couple of graves. I have brought them a long way back for burial but I have them all together and that is a great personal satisfaction to me. One of the things I have been able to do is to have all of my men properly gathered and buried in a central cemetery.

Jerry does seem to be pulling out here. It's a new experience for us to get ground without having to fight for it. Italy has a multitude of obstacles. The many rivers over which we have to put bridges slows down our progress. Often in this very wet weather, bridges that take days to build are washed away. I saw such a thing happen this morning. Water certainly has a power all its own!

October 28, 1944.

This has been a most uninteresting day. Our present location is by far the most unusual we have encountered. There is such a strange quietness in the air. I personally find it hard to believe we are actually in the line.

Early the C.O. and I took a walk along a very mucky road to see what our chances were of getting across the River Savio. It didn't take us long to find out that we had to remain on this side. We have troops on the other side and since I have one of my jobs to clear up, I was very anxious to get into one particular area. I'm afraid the evidence I really wanted has been washed away so it leaves me with a very difficult situation to clear up.

Just as dusk was setting in, one of our patrols brought in six prisoners. One of them, a young lad around 20, was wounded so I dressed his wound. He just arrived at supper time so we gave him something to eat and I watched him pack it away. It appears that he hadn't eaten for days. I took him to our hospital area and as we drove along we managed, in Italian, to exchange a few words. I found out that he was three years in the army and only one month in Italy. He told me that Hitler was finished and he was glad to be out of the war. I think many of them feel the same way. When I left him I gave him a smoke and he came smartly to attention and gave me our own salute.

October 29, 1944.

Another Sunday has come and gone and again because of our forward positions, I was unable to hold any services. Had the companies not been broken up I could hold a service somewhere since conditions are now on hold.

I did manage to pay a visit to all the companies. I found them all in good spirits and living high off the land. At one company there was a band of partisans. All they wanted to do was to kill Germans. They were really not very well organized. I noticed a lot of women among them all dressed like Christmas trees. I asked what they were doing and was told that they went out with the men to fight. I shouldn't wonder, after what I have seen here, that the Italian women would be great fighters. They seem to do *all* the work.

All week the Italians have been returning to their shattered homes. You feel very sorry for them, especially the children. I saw a little girl in a wagon and I mistook her for a doll. She was so sweet.

So far I think we have gone about as far as the weatherman will permit. It's absolutely impossible to move or pull off any major offensive in this kind of weather. If Jerry is pulling back, as we feel he has in our sector, we can always move along the main highways until we come across him. When we have to take to the open country then we are stuck. The best we can do here is to hold him from being used on other fronts.

I have just been called from the front to one of our rear hospitals to convey to a lad of our Unit the sad news of his brother's death. The mine that seriously wounded him, killed his brother. War is terribly cruel. When I got to where he was he had been moved farther back so I didn't get to see him.

November 1, 1944.

I'm back in the line tonight. There has been no change in our fighting situation since I left. It's just about the best go fighting men ever had. From all rumours it now appears we will be going to a rear area in a very few days.

After breakfast this morning I went out to a nearby mobile bath and gave myself the once over. I was awfully dirty. Tonight the M.O., a new one by the name of Duffy, who is substituting for Spafford, and I went to 'C' company for a grand duck supper. There was so much; I think we all had half a duck each.

The Telegram seems to keep everyone well informed of the goings on of the Irish. Bert Wemp, the war correspondent, is a very loyal supporter. He is always chasing us. Often I wonder how he comes to miss the odd shell. I remember last March he and I were having a chat by the side of the road when a few came over. For an old boy he moved for cover pretty fast, although I think I beat him!

All we seem to do these days is watch the waters rise and the mud grow muddier.

November 5, 1944.

We are now out for a rest period although our last time in was the best we have experienced in every way since we have been in action. We are presently situated in a very old town which has produced great men in Italian political, social and artistic life. For the time being George Duncan and I are living in a hotel. It's a fine spot where the beds are very comfortable and that is all that matters. We have a young Italian maid who brings us hot water to shave and generally does her best to keep the room spick and span.

In the course of a few days I expect to be making a complete visitation to the hospitals and that will take me anywhere from six to eight days. Right now our men are scattered all over the place and that makes tracking them down most difficult.

I went out to conduct a service for one of the companies. They are situated in an old monastery. I met a couple of monks who seemed rather glad to see me. One of them asked me if I was a Christian and when I told him that I was, he lifted my left hand and kissed my Irish ring.

November 6, 1944.

The old lady who runs this '*casa*' keeps coming into my room to have a chat with us. She has relatives in Canada and asks all kinds of questions about our country. This morning she brought us in some tea and afterwards hot water to shave. She tells us we are '*molto buono capitano.*'

Crawford Smith and I are sharing offices and so far most of our visitors have been Italians. They just come in to see if we have any thing to give away.

I expect to leave on Wednesday for seven days leave in Rome. Since we have come out of the line we have been favoured with good weather. It appears as if there has been a general slowing down on the front.

On Leave to Rome

November 9, 1944.

I was on the road from 9:00 a.m. yesterday until 7:00 p.m. last night. It was a long and tedious trip over roads that had many mud holes. As usual, Rome is a very busy place. The hotel is packed with officers, so I had difficulty in getting a room. When I came down to breakfast this morning, I met Ted and the educational lad and after we ate we drove around to see the sights. Ted, who occupies the room next door, was up in time to boil enough water for tea before the gas was turned off. The Romans just get gas about one hour at certain times of the day. The day is divided into four parts: early morning, noon, afternoon and evening. Since we have the complete use of a kitchen, we are able to put a quick breakfast together. The total price for the day is one good Canadian dollar!

There seems to be plenty in the shops here but the Roman shopkeepers tend to be a bit roguish, so I'll save my money until I get home. According to the Maple Leaf, our army newspaper, General McNaughton has arranged for home leaves for Christmas for long service men. It won't include me since it applies to men away from Canada for four or five years.

I took in a very good show in the afternoon, '*As Thousands Cheer.*' It certainly provided a real lift to my spirits.

November 15, 1944.

About an hour ago I arrived back from Rome. I was on the road from 8:00 a.m. until 7:00, so tonight after travelling all that way (220 miles) in an army vehicle, I'm like a man without insides! I had a pretty good leave and the change I know, will do me some measure of good. During my leave I was able to attend an international soccer match between England and Poland. It did bring back some old memories. I was also taken to visit the Palace of the Dorias. The Princess personally took me on a sight-seeing tour and I fail to find words to describe all I saw.

I heard today that my cousin Roy from Oxford is missing, presumed killed. He was in the recent airborne invasion in Holland. Aunt Ethel is most distraught. This war is certainly exacting it's toll on human lives.

I received a telegram from Cooke's Presbyterian Church in Toronto asking me if I would accept a call. Of course, it's impossible but I thought it was nice of them to think of me.

November 16, 1944.

Today I had a number of interviews. They kind of piled up since my leave. If we were to send every man home who has a problem, our ranks would be depleted. Of course, you can't blame the poor lads. I think after the war I will set up a domestic relations office. I believe I could make a pretty good living! My years in the army have given me the answers to many human problems.

I have a great deal of correspondence to get off. My next-of-kin requests are very difficult. Their questions are heartbreaking. Did he ask for the children? Did he mention my name? Did he have my ring on? All these despite the fact that I have told them that he was killed instantly. Poor souls have so much sorrow that it just drives them to want to know all they can. They have all my concern and care, and I pray I may never become superficial or unthoughtful. It must be terrible to lose one you love in such a tragic way.

November 18, 1944.

The armies on the western fronts are on the move again. According to today's news they all had taken their first objectives. This may be the beginning of the push that will take them right into the heart of Germany.

War at the moment is far removed for us. Resting as we are, we have erased all thoughts of war from our minds. It is a comfortable feeling. Under these conditions precious little of any importance happens. You just eat and sleep and attend to the normal army duties that come your way. One thing that we are attempting for the men is an intensive educational programme. If the plan works the men will benefit greatly. It is really part of the rehabilitation process in order to assist the men to get back quickly and easily into civilian life. It's encouraging to know the government is making some attempt, even before the war is over to prepare the soldier to return to civilian life. We don't want a repeat of the days following the last war.

November 21, 1944.

I spent most of my day enrolling lads for the educational subjects. The response has far exceeded anything I expected. So far I have some 300 in the Unit who want to improve their minds. Most of the subjects are at the elementary level. There are a few who are anxious to finish their junior or senior matriculation. It's rather interesting to note how they are swinging toward languages. By far the most popular are French, Italian and German.

We are fortunate in our Unit to have some dozen officers who are competent teachers, the majority of them with university degrees. I have noticed most of the newer and younger officers coming in are university men. Over the past year, most of them have come right out of school into the army. Needless to say the lads will have a lot of things to learn. Like the rest of us, it won't take them long.

Our rest area is developing into a pretty enjoyable spot for the lads. Plenty of shows, concerts and dances going on. I have managed to get a library going. It's remarkable how many there are (according to the books taken out) who must be spending their spare time reading. Since it now looks like we will be spending Christmas in Italy, we all hope we manage to remain right here. Already some of the five year men are being organized to get them back to Canada by Christmas. Since we have only a few who are qualified, they are most anxious to get home.

Tomorrow we are anticipating with interest what may happen in Canada's House of Commons. Naturally, we feel heads will roll over the Ralston situation. It's too bad those in authority can't be more sensible about the needs of the army. Manpower is needed and whether Quebec agrees or not we have to get men to finish off this war.

November 22, 1944.

I'm anxiously waiting for the 9:00 p.m. news to see if anything startling occurred in Canada's House of Commons today. No doubt the 'Zombie' question came up and I'm wondering if the House is really brave enough to force them to go active.

The 'Zombie' attitude is causing no end of dissension among the troops over here. It's too bad that division and strife is growing in our Dominion when we should all be united. As far as I'm concerned, Canada has much to teach the rest of the world and it would be unfortunate if anything, of a political or religious nature, should hinder such a needed programme. I know when I throw open my 'Padre's Hour' for general questions, I never fail to hear the following: "What are we going to do with Quebec?"" What does she think of her isolation?" I feel the solution is in the hands of any government brave enough to value federal unity over political party policies.

This morning at 10:00 a.m. I went for a second sitting on myself. I'm having my portrait painted. It's all very funny. You go into the artist's house or studio for a couple of hours and just sit. Sometimes she lets me walk around so she can pick out some features. She is always talking about capturing or arresting features. When she gets what she wants she seems quite elated. At the rate she is going, it will take me about six two hour sittings to get my head and shoulders on canvas. I told her that I'm having it painted for my wife so she had better do an extra fine job. She was doing my eyes today and told me that she thought I had a bit of the devil in them!

This afternoon I was off playing football. The way I feel tonight I know I must be getting to be a very old man. We won and that made the lads on the team very happy.

November 24, 1944.

According to the radio reports we are getting, there is quite a bit of excitement going on in Ottawa. We hear some 16,000 men will be sent overseas whether they like it or not. Air Minister Powers apparently doesn't like the idea, so has resigned. Before the whole debate is over, it might not be a bad idea if they all packed up and went home instead of making a laughing stock out of Canada in general, and in particular out of the lads who have done a good job serving our nation. The present crisis in our government gives the impression that we are a bunch of *'pikers'* having no interest in a complete and decisive defeat over the enemy. The influence of Quebec and her apparent hatred for things British, gives a questionable impression to the rest of the Allies. The sooner she realizes that she is part of the Dominion and must share equally the responsibilities, the better it will be for her and the rest of the provinces. I suppose we shouldn't get too hot over these things, but one despairs to see all the effort being shouldered by eight provinces, while the other gets off free and enjoys making a comfortable living at the expense of the faithful volunteer.

There appears to be great progress being made against the Hun. The present operations in France are going beyond expectations. Should the Hun decided to stand and fight this side of the Rhine, I think he can be licked before the end of the year. If he retires to the other side, it can last until next spring.

December 2, 1944.

There are only 22 more shopping days left until Christmas! It would be wonderful if I could say that there are only 22 more days left of this horrible war.

We have now left our resting place and are in the line once again. It seems strange to be within the sound and shake of the guns for another time. Our period of rest was by far the best. Not only the lads but the civilians were sorry to see it come to an end. Crawford and I had quite the send-off by our landlady. She was really brokenhearted to see us go. The tears that she shed and the handshakes were most genuine. We had to get out quickly before we broke down ourselves. I'm quite sure that the old lady and her husband couldn't have said goodby any better or more affectionately to their sons. We have a standing invitation to return. She promised to keep our room and said that she would not let any other soldier occupy it.

We were on the road all day yesterday and again today. Fortunately the weather was in our favour. Today the sun shone like it would in July. We got into the line without any casualties and even though we are in action I pray we will have no fatal ones. With the end of hostilities in sight, I don't want to see any of our lads getting hurt.

Here We Go Again

December 3, 1944.

After the comfortable rest period, I haven't got down to front line soldiering. These past couple of nights I have had a real hard job getting off to sleep. I suppose I have too much personal comfort.

Things are going along just fine. We got through the night without any unusual disturbances. I pray we do this job without any serious injury. The weather is not too good. Nonetheless we managed to get a pretty good house for our R.A.P. ...; we are not too badly off. The Italians here are very helpful. The Hun treated them pretty badly, hence they are quick to assist us in order that we may get at Jerry.

December 6, 1944.

I am setting up in a comfortable R.A.P. where a grand wood fire is burning. The M.O. has just gone off to sleep. I thought I would sit up a little while in case any casualties come in. So far we have been doing extremely well.

The lads are making fine progress. The Canadian soldier does an excellent job. There has never been an objective assigned them that they have failed to take. I can recall an English brigade making two attempts to take Coriano and failing both times. We did it in three days. That's why one gets so mad at fellows back home rebelling because they are being sent overseas. One would think if they had any backbone they would want to come over and be part of such an important cause. I'm afraid the lads will have a lot of nasty things to say to them when they do get back.

We came into town this morning and you would have thought it was the 'Glorious Twelfth'. The Italians came out in the hundreds giving us a real welcome. Some of the lads me thinks, took too much of the 'vino'. The partisans particularly are here to assist us. They are very helpful when we have a town or piece of country to clean up. They know all the houses where the Hun is located!

December 7, 1944.

The situation is well in hand. The going has been very good and our success quite satisfactory. We are hopeful the dent we have made in his line will help to push the German a bit nearer home and hasten our speedy evacuation of this country. One of the happy features of this operation is the speed with which we travel along. We never seem to stay very long in one spot. So far we have attended to more wounded civilians than to our own men. Some of these people take too many unnecessary chances and as a result all too many of them are being hurt. The old people and children get all our sympathy. They aren't responsible for any of this.

It will be a very happy day when this unnecessary wastage of human life and property shall cease. War has a way of destroying all human values. It puts a queer bend in one's thinking. I shouldn't wonder that a few months after it's over our thinking will straighten itself out.

I often wonder as I sit in these dilapidated Italian houses, how long I must wait before I will occupy my own comfortable home. I do believe, however, that the picture for the future is very bright. Despite the fact there is still a lot of fighting ahead, I don't think we will be at it much longer.

I had twenty replies today from loved ones who were now officially notified that their missing ones are prisoners in Germany. I'm only hoping that all those whom I reported to loved ones as suspected prisoners of war, will turn up.

December 10, 1944.

I have now received 45 letters from relatives who have been notified that their loved ones are prisoners of war. That just leaves ten to go and I'm sure they too will be among the rest. Wives and mothers are certainly happy and their letters are full of praise and thanksgiving. Some of their letters are really masterpieces. There are so many who wish to see me on my return, that I must save these replies to know where to find them. It is important that I do the job properly.

This was no more like Sunday than Christmas is like Easter. Our war machine was busy grinding the enemy down and pushing him a bit farther north. War, with it's constant urgency, gives little time to stop and pay respect to holy days. One's meditation in the line is certainly done in private. I trust God will forgive our stupidity and our enemy, who has deprived so many of the practice of public worship.

From all my correspondence received to date, there are just five men unaccounted for. I'm hopeful I will get a perfect score. This is the first time prisoners of war have been reported so quickly.

Our sleep was disturbed early this morning. Some of the lads got caught in a minefield. All of them were amputation cases. Mines certainly make an awful mess of the human body. It's a cruel and inhuman way to fight a war. Despite their wounds, the poor lads were wonderful to work on. Most of them will come through all right.

December 12, 1944.

I have been on the go constantly. The boys have chased the Hun so fast we have been on wheels most of the past 48 hours. Strangely enough our casualties are never quite so high when we are advancing.

The weather so far has not hindered our progress. It's amazing how men can grab off a little sleep under such conditions. The Canadian soldier is indeed making a name for himself. He is superior in making bridge heads and as a spearhead fighter there are none better. I only hope on their return to Canada, good and adequate provision will be made for their adjustment to civilian life. I'd hate to think of such fine sacrifice and noble courage being in anyway neglected or overlooked.

The present political crisis in Canada over the 'Zombie' question discredits our political leaders and leaves us here wondering what has gone wrong with our young Canadian manhood. If ever lads on the battlefront took the attitude so openly displayed by Canada's 'Zombies', the Hun would soon be heading for our shores. Thank God that will never be the case!

December 13, 1944.

This has been a very tough and tedious day. The day was damp and wet hence visibility was poor for our fighting machine. Our planes help our forward troops when they can get going but the lads are on their own at the moment.

Jerry has been able to take advantage of weather conditions so we have been getting a stiff bit of shelling. Fortunately it has not done us much harm, apart from disturbing our sleep. When one comes over, you brace yourself ready to take cover if it hits the house. They have all missed. The infantry soldier has the toughest assignment. He walks for miles through mud and rain. When he comes to a river and the bridge is blown, he just has to swim or wade across. In the past few days our lads have done a lot of that kind of thing. In spite of the obstacles, they push on, killing or capturing the enemy. They are a grand lot of fighting men!

According to our army newspaper Mitch Hepburn is again leader of the Ontario Liberals. Surely they must be in tough shape when they have to call him back into office.

I had a long talk with Ray Boyden this afternoon. He was quite excited since he was just awarded the D.S.O. He has done an excellent job. Our C.O. got his this week ... recognition for the fine effort the Unit has made. A number of the lads got M.M.'s.

December 14, 1944.

It is quiet this evening so possibly I will be able to sleep without having to run for cover, as I had in the past few evenings. On getting back to 'civvie street' I am sure I will enjoy being able to sit down with a decent electric light on, in a comfortable chair, and do some reading or writing. While the present gets pretty black and dull at times, the future always has a bright sun in the sky.

I laid two of my lads away today. It's always hard to see our fine young men paying such a price. I'm afraid it will be a sorrowful Christmas for many Canadian households.

On the whole our operations are going very well. A break in the weather would help us a lot. When we left the mountains we thought our troubles would be over. Now we have river crossings to contend with every few miles.

December 15, 1944.

I am having a 24 hour rest from the line tonight. While I'm not too far away, I'm still far enough to miss Jerry's shells and so should catch a good night's sleep. This has been one of Italy's perfect days. Around eight the sun came out with a blast and remained until late this evening, thus providing an opportunity for our planes to put on the pressure. They seemed to be dropping bombs on Jerry all day. I was glad I was on our side of the line. It's strange how one delights in seeing the enemy get it. The lads just cheered as wave after wave of 'spits' went in to empty their loads of destruction.

I laid away a couple of my fine lads this morning. Both were killed by snipers. I grieve to think we must continue to lose men at this late date.

December 17, 1944.

Our rest period has been extended to another 24 hours. None of us do anything but approve. Of course the sooner we get going and capture our final objective the sooner we will be out of the line again. According to the news we got today we have now six armies fighting on German soil. I only pray they move as fast through Germany as they did through France. While it was Sunday I was unable to hold any services. I took the opportunity of visiting my lads graves and erecting white crosses on them. Our cemeteries are quite nice amd I must say the Italians love to come and put flowers on the graves.

I managed to call on a few lads in detention and I think I convinced two of them to get out and play the game. Some of the poor lads get kind of shaky in battle and under fire go to pieces. At the time they do things they wouldn't do under ordinary circumstances.

December 22, 1944.

I've managed about 5 hours sleep in the last 48 hours. We have just finished a pretty severe battle. Again we proved too much for the Hun and drove him back another five or six miles. I spent all day yesterday on our battlefield. The Jerry chased me a few times with his shelling, but before dark came I had all my lads gathered up and safely put away in a house where I picked them up this morning and took them for burial to Villanova, a very nice Canadian cemetery. I'm pretty weary of all this bloodshed. As I moved over the battlefield I prayed to God to bring us to the end of it all. 'Tis a strange contrast to see the enemy dead and our own, lying side by side. God, I know, made us to be friends and one man has made us into enemies. I'm afraid many families will just be sitting down to their Christmas dinner when the sad news will arrive. Many poor souls find it hard and difficult to understand. One has to remain bright and cheery despite the things that one sees and does.

December 23, 1944.

Today reminded me of Canada. We had our first snow and while it is not going to stay very long, it was still a grand sight. Anything is better than the rain we get in this country. If the ground would only firm up it would make the going much better and easier for our lads. It's terrible to see them ploughing through mud and rivers, and lying for long periods in water-filled ditches waiting to get at the enemy. It takes some endurance but they stick to it and successfully do their job. The infantry soldier is certainly the backbone of the army. His task is quite the grimmest and most difficult in modern warfare.

We are going to have our Christmas dinner in the lines. Funny place and a funny way to spend such an all important event.

December 24, 1944.

It's Christmas eve. The clock has reached the hour of 9:00 p.m. The boys in the R.A.P. are doing their best to be as happy as possible. Wine and the contents of Christmas parcels are going the rounds. All are trying to think about what is going on around the family circle tonight.

The absence of shot and shell may indicate neither side is anxious to destroy, at least for tonight, the real peace of our very hallowed Christmas Eve. While we have to be in the line for tonight, I'm praying that our Christmas may not be darkened by casualties of any kind. I hope it is not too much to expect. We are going to have plenty to eat and drink. The M.O. and I are going to be the special cooks and serve our Christmas meal. The lads on the R.A.P. staff are really going to have one big holiday. I really didn't think that I would be spending another Christmas in Italy. Tonight I again count my many blessings.

December 25, 1944.

Although in the line we did have a fine Christmas, the day was warm and very clear. No snow of any kind fell. The M.O. and I got up at seven and prepared the breakfast for the staff. We gave them buttered toast, sausages, spam and nice hot tea. For dinner we prepared a pork roast, mashed potatoes with nice brown gravy, plum pudding and hot tea. We opened our Christmas parcels and from them handed out some very nice extras.

To make the day a little more pleasant, our casualties were light and there was very little shelling. I suppose by tomorrow we will be at it again. My, but it all is so very foolish! What a way to settle our international arguments! I wonder how long it will take us to come to our senses.

December 27, 1944.

Tonight we are having a rest from the line. Guess we may have the opportunity of New Year's Day all to ourselves. Just to get a chance to have a wash, haircut and bath will be a real treat. I'm long overdue at the moment.

We had an exceptionally good night. The only thing that disturbed us was a few Jerry shells that landed close to our buildlng. I got a few pieces of shrapnel through my caravan. Since I wasn't in it there was nothing to worry about. We don't worry much about such things anyway.

Our location for our short breather is pretty good. I only wish they thought about a heating system for their homes in this country. We are getting quite a few frosty nights and mornings. During the day the sun gets fairly warm.

December 28, 1944.

Today we were again favoured with a sunny day. I called in the morning at one of our nearby hospitals to see some of the lads. All of them had lost legs and I still can't figure out why they are so cheerful. Possibly the idea of home and the end of their fighting days may have much to do with it. In the afternoon I buried one of the lads who had died of wounds. No matter how you look at it, physical disabilities are going to present real difficulties in civilian life. Such men should be given a very high pension on their return.

From the front came better news today. We heard the German advance had been halted. We now are looking for a cutoff manoeuvre and then I believe the Hun will have had it. None the less he is very daring and anxious to hold on. We can never expect to have him properly licked until our armies overrun Germany and take full possession of that country.

December 30, 1944.

As you can see there is just one more day left in this year. I can't say I'm sorry to see this year pass away. As we know, it's been a year full of war, destruction and loss of life. It's truly a year I want to erase from my mind. 1944 has nothing but sorrow associated with it. When I think of the many homes, mothers, wives and children, whose lives have been saddened by the Messenger of Death, I'd gladly bury 1944 in the deepest grave I could find.

We look on the new year to bring us victory and an end to this awful conflict. I feel confident that 1945 will bring more joy and gladness. I am sure it will see me home and what more in this life could I ask for.

Tonight the Regiment had their Christmas and New Year's dinner. It was a huge success. The lads had plenty of turkey, pudding, beer and fruit. They were a very happy crowd, and they left the building with big broad grins on their faces. It doesn't take much to make us happy these days. I'm sure the lads got a kick out of being waited on by officers.

This is actually my fifth Christmas with the Regiment. I'm one of the old timers now. There are not many who started with me. Since it's going to be my last year in the army, I've reason to rejoice. I'll just go on counting the days until I'm home.

December 31, 1944.

It's the last day of the old year. Although it's late evening, I don't think I'll sit up to wait the arrival of 'Baby 1945'. I can recall how often, before this war came along, we would wait for the New Year. On every veranda voices would shout, car horns would blow and factories would sound their whistles. Somehow the old zest for such wholesome merriment has gone. It's a pretty serious world we live in. It's hard for people back home to be happy when every hour of their day is filled with anxiety.

What a release to all our hearts when we know the noise of battle has disappeared and our world is assured of a lasting peace. This morning, I held a service for the lads. We sang Christmas carols. The men love to sing them. The service was held in a large, cold theatre, not too conducive to public worship. There were 160 missing faces. Lads who last year sang with the rest, but now take their place in the congregation of God.

I took my sermon from Joshua 1: 9. Indeed the whole nine verses are inspirational and offer the kind of help we need as we go into action. I'm coming to feel more and more how much I daily need the presence of Christ in my life. There is so little here. His presence means so much. I believe my experience has put a little more iron in my faith and I have learned to depend just a bit more upon the gracious promises of God. He certainly has delivered me from some difficult situations during the year.

Italy 1945

January 1, 1945.

Despite the fact that I didn't plan to sit up and welcome the New Year, I did. Six of the lads and myself sat around an old oil stove in a very cold Italian room in Ravenna and did our best to give the *'little fellow'* our blessing when he came through the open door. On his arrival, we gathered around, looked at each other and agreed to christen him *'Victory'*. I read Psalm 91 and with the prayer in our hearts that this new year would see us through to the finish, we went off to bed. I'm writing this from the lines; a rather strange way to start a new year. Just goes to show what men have to do when they get into a war. As far as the weather is concerned, the day is pretty good. The cold helps to firm up the ground and adds to our advantage. Tanks can keep on going and that's great music to an infantry man's ears!

January 2, 1945.

I'm a little tired tonight and didn't manage to get any sleep during the night. We have been quite busy all day. We are having a quiet spell at the moment in the R.A.P. and, while it is 10:00 p.m., I'm hoping I can finish my writing withoUt any interruption.

As usual, the lads are doing a grand job. They must have captured 100 prisoners today. We attended to a good number of enemy wounded, and from the way they responded to our treatment I shouldn't wonder but they were surprised. I think they are told, when they fall into the hands of the Canadians, they are immediately shot. One lad in the R.A.P. who can speak German, was told by one of the enemy wounded, that Canadians were better to them than they had been told. I often wonder how much longer their propaganda will keep them going. These fellows were very poorly dressed and as I was giving one a cup of tea, I thought he would eat the hands off me! They were terribly hungry. Like ourselves they carry snaps of their loved ones. They like you to see them. Possibly they think they must to gain sympathy.

January 5, 1945.

I have been terribly busy. I have passed through a real hell these past two days. Tonight I have found myself a quiet corner where I hope I can have some time to think.

One of the sad blows of the operation was the death of the M.O. and the medical sergeant. I laid them away today and I don't think I have quite gotten over the shock of it. The R.A.P. got a direct hit and both of them were killed instantly. I have worked and lived with them for so long that we were like brothers. The M.O.'s wife is presently in England and I know it's going to be a terrible shock to her. They were only married a couple of years and had great plans for the future. He was a grand lad (just 27) and I'm going to miss his comradeship very much. The sergeant, too, had just been awarded the MM for his work at Coriano. It's a blow that hurts deeply.

How I pray to God that it may end soon, before we must lose more fine and wonderful lads. I'm afraid the successes achieved against the enemy mean very little to me right at the moment.

January 6, 1945.

Yesterday I felt very discouraged. Today I feel a little better. It's wonderful what a good night's sleep does to a tired mind and body. We have gone 48 hours without any casualties and that is always good news.

For the first time in a couple of weeks we are having a very wet day. The way the mud has taken possession of the area you'd think it had rained for weeks. Funny old country this Italy. I believe I'll be happy to leave it. We got a new M.O. today by the name of Duffy. He's a pretty good sort. I still can't believe that Bill Spafford is gone.

I was out visiting the lads at their outposts. Since we have had a whole day's rain, the mud was in layers right up to my knees. It's difficult to imagine men in slit trenches half full of water protecting the ground they have gained. What men go through for the victory and peace is worthy of the highest praise. The comforts of home will indeed have a great appeal to us now. I'm afraid many of us didn't appreciate all that was ours when back in Canada.

Fortunately we have been free of any casualties this past 24 hours. It's a blessing when we are able to avoid them. It will be a delight when we know the last shot is fired, the last man wounded, the last comrade killed. It will be a day of great personal joy.

January 9, 1945.

Last night was perfect. We went through the whole night without even the noise of battle. Around the R.A.P., that is always an occasion for great relief and personal joy.

Today was very bright. We had a little snow on the ground, hence we felt more like Canadians. A mobile bath moved in this afternoon close to the R.A.P. so I went over and had a real wash-down. I also got a complete change of underwear. It certainly adds to one's personal comfort.

I was around to see one of the companies. The lads were busy cutting up a calf and they invited me to stay for dinner. If the front line is not too interesting, it still affords the lads the opportunity to have a change of diet. At one of the sections where the Germans had left behind some horses and wagons, the lads had one all rigged up and were taking little drives across the fields. I had a go but the horse wanted to go home to his masters and I had a bit of a job getting him turned around. I guess a German horse is not to be trusted too far!

Our new M.O. and I are getting along very well together, although I still find it hard to believe that Bill Spafford has gone. Everytime I come into the R.A.P. I expect to see him ... I worked so long and so well with him we naturally became very close friends.

January 13, 1945.

Looking back over my diary, I find we are in the line exactly one year tonight. I can remember how awfully green we all were. We don't take the chances now that we did then. We have come a long way. A year ago tonight we were sitting waiting to go into the attack at Ortona. Tonight we are well north of Ravenna, possibly a distance of 300 miles. It's been a long hard grind and the cost in human life has been devastating. I often think of the many homes from our own Regiment that have been made sad. It has been a very trying year for loved ones. While the end does not appear to be very near, it nevertheless is not too far off.

I had to go out and bury a couple of lads and was thoroughly soaked when I returned to the R.A.P. I got into bed and didn't wake up until the morning. I have been trying to get some next-of-kin letters off. My, but I will be so happy when such things come to an end for me. Right now reinforcements are arriving pretty quickly. I have talked to a good number of lads in our Unit who were in Canada in November and December. Some of them have already paid with their lives. I buried a good number of lads this time, who only spent one day or night in the line.

January 22, 1945.

We are finally out of the line. We are well-located and if it were only summertime we could be spending some time swimming in the Adriatic, we are so close. While not everything they might be, our billets are comfortable. I am personally fixed up quite nicely in a private home. The old lady is extremely clean and gave me the best and most convenient room in the house. She put her best furniture in the room and the bed is almost too comfortable. Before I get up she has a nice cup of tea ready for me. Since she knows I'm a padre, she has erected a very large picture over my bed of Joseph, Mary and Jesus on their way to Jerusalem. She means well and we are getting along famously.

We got word today that Warsaw had fallen and the Russlans had made a breakthrough. The latest reports indicate that they are only 15 miles from the German border. I trust it may prove a quick answer to all our prayers. It would be wonderful if we didn't have to go back into the line. Personally I have had enough of the war.

January 23, 1945.

Are we excited this morning! News came in that the Russians are 165 miles from Berlin. A three-hour ride and going strong! The old sun of hope is shining very brightly this a.m. Wouldn't it be wonderful if this advance turned out to be the final push of the war! I'm rather hoping that the Russian army gets to Berlin before we do. I feel they know better than we, how to treat the Hun. They have seen what he did in their country, so should know how to deal with him when they arrive.

I see by the papers back home that I was mentioned in despatches. I really don't know how that came about. I haven't seen the citation myself. I suppose it was something I did last winter. The most heroic thing that I did was run like the devil with my pants down when a shell dropped very close. I really don't take any unnecessary chances.

Things are going pretty well in the rest area. Last night I got all my next-of-kin letters finished. I have quite a pile and it's a relief to have them completed.

Our C.O. is preparing to leave us. I hear he won't be coming back. He has been on the go steadily for over a year, and is now pretty well worn out. He's not so young anymore; however, he has done an excellent job. Leigh Payne is taking over at the moment. I would like to see him get the Unit.

We are enjoying our rest very much. So far I haven't managed to share in much of it. Just seems I have a hundred and one things to do. I hope to have my desk clear by the end of the week so I can get off to the hospitals. I'm also hoping to score a few day's leave.

January 27, 1945.

The freedom of a rear rest has it's effects on us all. Here lights and fires burn unhindered. There is no Hun close enough to detect our whereabouts. This morning we said good-by to our C.O. He left us for places unknown. He gave us an excellent farewell speech and indeed was sorry to have to go. He has completed a good tour of duty with the Regiment, and brought us through some trying times. Leigh Payne takes over and he too will do a good job. Being an imaginative Irishman, he naturally gets the full cooperation and support of our ranks.

January 31, 1945.

Our war prospects are brighter today than they were a year ago. Our news this morning tells us the Russians are only 80 miles from Berlin. They will soon have it tucked away in their bag of captured German cities. The drive has also begun in the west, and indications are that all armies there will push on till they contact the Russians. In the midst of it all, our front fades. It matters little where the action takes place so long as it means the destruction of the enemy and the quick end of this cursed war.

The powers that be are giving me a rest. On Monday February 5th, I'm to report for duty at a General Hospital in Rome. I'm to remain there for a couple of months and then return to the Unit. All of this means I won't be going into the next action with the Irish. The story is that I've put more time in the lines than anyone else. In fact, I'm the only one in the Unit who has actually been in all engagements. Officers and men get turns at being left out of battle. Since I have gotten a full year in, they are going to give me a rest.

I'm holding a special memorial service on Sunday, so today I spent time trying to get it organized. I'm having a special order of service prepared and I can tell you that working with an Italian printer presents many problems. Tomorrow I'm going to get my things packed for Rome. It's going to be quite a change. I don't know if I'll like it.

February 2, 1945.

Today I was busy getting all my files cleaned up. I want to have everything in shape before I pull out. So far Capt. Williams, who is to relieve me, has not shown up. I wanted to be here for our memorial service tomorrow. Maybe by Monday or Tuesday I'll be ready to go.

Yesterday I received my oak leaf from the King so I got my Italian landlady to sew it on. She wanted to know what it was for, so I told her it was for capturing 50 Huns. She almost kissed me! Don't I have fun! Tonight she is cooking the M.O. and I our dinner. We got a turkey for the occasion so it should feed us all all right.

February 4, 1945.

This morning we held our memorial service and a very impressive service it was. Our pipe band added much dignity and solemnity to the occasion. After the service we had a march past and C.O. Leigh Payne took the salute. He invited me to the stand along with him. I said it seemed a bit unusual, but he replied that he was an unusual C.O. So there I was looking very military while the troops filed by.

This afternoon the senior chaplain called to tell me to be ready to move by Wednesday. I'm afraid the ease and comfort of a hospital chaplain will get me down for a while. The way things are going now, it's difficult to predict what will happen. The end may come very, very, soon.

February 7, 1945.

I spent most of my time in Ravenna today. It was a long and tiresome trip, especially since the highway was crowded with convoys. I had a few things to clear up with the boss-chaplain before leaving for Rome which I hope to do around 9:00 a.m. tomorrow.

Today was just like another spring. As I drove along the highway I noticed the farmers ploughing in their fields. They use oxen. One man holds the plough and another out in front, seems to be literally dragging the old oxen along. It reminds me of the scenes one sees around Quebec. The women are trying to rebuild and patch up their broken-down homes. The Hun had certainly made the Italian pay dearly for changing sides.

I see where General McNaughton lost the election. Possibly the Canadian people have advanced the point of view held by so many in the armed services. As a result of the 'Zombie' question, the lads feel they have been badly let down. It's good that it hasn't affected the progress of the war. At the present time everything looks good.

February 9, 1945.

I have just arrived at my new job. I left the Unit yesterday morning and since it was slightly over 200 miles, I was on the road all day. I didn't arrive at the hospital until 8:00 p.m. Ted drove me down, but I did take my turn behind the wheel. Fortunately the day was perfect. The roads over the mountains were in good shape and traffic was very light.

The old Italian landlady couldn't quite understand my departure. I got the usual Italian farewell ... lots of tears and plenty of handshakes. They are certainly an emotional people. Ted returned to the Unit this morning. He didn't like the idea of my going ... says he's afraid he won't get along with the new padre. He has been very loyal to me. Many times, after a battle, he has helped me with situations that were not very pleasant to deal with. I would have liked to have him with me here but since my stay will only be for a month I couldn't arrange it.

Today I was like a fish out of water. Just didn't know how to act, or show interest in what I was suppose to do. To break myself in, I went around all the wards and looked up all my Irish lads. I found about 15 of them. One lad in particular, who had lost both legs, was a real inspiration. The first thing ke said to me was "Padre, you made a good job of cutting my leg off." I remember when he came to the R.A.P.; his leg was lying loose in his boot and I removed it. He was so bright and cheerful I came away much better as a result of our visit.

February 12, 1945.

Here I am back with the Unit! My stay at the hospital was very brief. It was a pretty decent set-up. I had a steam heated room and hot and cold water in the bathroom. When the messenger arrived at my room I had not unpacked any of the gear, so got away light on that score. I ran up to the hotel to see if any of the officers were around who were going back by car but didn't have any luck. Next, I had to make arrangements to come back by train. Sunday at 1:00 p.m., I got on my first Italian train and headed north. The trip was long but comfortable. I got to my destination this morning at 9:30 a.m. no one knew I was coming, so I was in a bit of a fix since the Unit was some twenty miles away and couldn't be reached by phone, I left my baggage at the station and started to hitchhike. I hadn't gone far till I was picked up and got to where I was going on time. When I arrived and walked into the office, the boys nearly had a fit. They heard the new padre was arriving today, but it turned out to be the old one. While the set up in the hospital was as perfect as one could expect, my two days there convinced me I'd sooner be with the Regiment. One doesn't get the same personal contact. Men just seem to come and go, hence you really never get to know them. At least I had a good visit with my own lads, so my trip wasn't quite in vain.

I heard from Mrs. Spafford and poor soul doesn't know what to make of Bill's death. She knew that we were always together and was afraid to write for she thought I might have been with him. As a matter of fact, it was the first time he ever went forward without me, and this was because I had to go out and bury a lad.

Belgium 1945

March 5, 1945.

We have been on the move since February 13 and were not permitted to write anything during our travels. I'm a lot closer to home than I have been in a long time and I pray that it won't be long before I'll be home altogether. I'm writing this letter from Belgium and I can say without reservation, that it is a wonderful change. It's like coming out of the cellar into the living room. Everyone is so clean and so nice it's almost like being in some parts of Canada. We are billeted out in private homes and the people are absolutely wonderful. At the moment I'm living in the home of the parish priest. He speaks a little English so we get along pretty well. Our officers' mess is in the town pub, so you can visualize the situation. It's all such a wonderful contrast that I love it. I have seen some excellent cities, towns and villages ... places that I use to read about in history classes. In the course of a few days I am going on leave to England. I'm planning to go up to Oxford. I know that my aunt would like to have me, and since they have lost Roy I think a visit from me might help.

March 6, 1945.

I am still enjoying the change of location. I moved yesterday from the parish priest's to a Belgium family where I'm now staying. They call us their liberators and for some reason the Canadian soldier is tops in their estimation. I think the Canadians went on their advance through this particular part. The mother always wants to feed you. Before I was out of bed this morning I was presented with tea and toast. Tonight, she insisted I have supper with them. They drink beer with their meals and couldn't understand why I didn't partake. We are having the usual fun learning their language. Already I have picked up a few household words. They speak Flemish and it sounds almost like German. One of the sons, who speaks English pretty well, is teaching me the 'lingo'. I spent most of the day visiting the companies. As in England they are located in small towns and villages. I found all enjoying themselves to the full. Most of the men have private homes to live in and are treated like kings.

Tonight the first group of men left for England. They included men whose wives and families were there. You should have seen their faces when they pulled out. The village we are in is certainly a grand one. It's nice to go walking down its clean streets. The little children love to stop you to speak and shake your hand. Already the citizens of the village are arranging dances and entertainment for the lads. In many ways it is like things were when we were in England although the people may be more friendly. If not for the language difficulty we would be having a whale of a time.

March 8, 1945.

There is quite a bit of excitement around this part of the world tonight. Allied troops are across the Rhine. Such a move is regarded as highly important. It may now hasten the end. I pray it may be so for I do long to get home.

I'm afraid that all I've done today is interview men who desire to get married on their leaves to England. They are a very excited bunch of lads. I told one lad (kidding of course) that he couldn't get married and so help me, he nearly broke down and cried. I thought I'd better not carry my joke too far or something serious might happen. When I told him that I was kidding, he said, "Padre, you are an awful man." Some of them seem so very young. I often wonder how they will make out.

March 10, 1945.

This has been a rather interesting day. I spent all of it going over the battlefields of the last war. I started my tour with a guide from the city of Ypres. This city, apparently well-known to our Canadian fathers, has so many places of interest it is difficult to name them all. The gate to the city, which is a memorial tower, has some 40,000 names inscribed upon it ... a good number of them are Canadian. From the city I drove to places like "Hill 60-62" and to a woods that still has the trenches of 1914-18. I visited about six cemeteries, all of them nicely kept. Not one of them had less than a couple of thousand graves. One thing struck me — the very large number of unknown dead. I never did think such a condition existed. Our record in this war is very much better. Out of the 180 dead in Italy, there was only one I was unable to find and he was blown to pieces beside a river which carried his body away. Even then I managed to find some of his letters and clothing. After viewing this loss of human life one would have thought another war such as we are fighting today, could never have started. The Hun surely must have a short memory.

March 11, 1945.

Today I was very busy. The Regiment is broken up into companies, each company having a small village all to itself. It's necessary to hold services by company arrangement. I covered three companies today; two this morning and one this afternoon. I took along the pipe band and so help me the young and old in each village turned out in the hundreds. The band played about fifteen minutes in each village and when they finished the people cheered and clapped. They seem to like the pipes. One village where we have no soldiers, is quite annoyed about it so they have requested the band to play their village as soon as possible.

This is a strong Roman Catholic country and we have no Protestant churches hence we use the men's mess or the schoolrooms for our services. All of them are very comfortable, so it works out quite nicely.

I have arranged to have dinner with Bill Elder. He's got a very fine set up. Now that he is a major, I try to give him a little more respect!

March 13, 1945.

I think Belgium must be getting it's spring. Today it is warm as toast and all the villagers are out in their small gardens putting in their seeds. Already I noticed a good number of spring flowers showing their heads. At the home where I'm staying, they have quite a nice garden and in it there is a perfect border of primroses, out in all kinds of colour. In many ways this country reminds me of England. They seem to do things the same way and have a healthy respect for the English. When the soldiers were here in '40 the people did a great deal for them and when they had to get out they gave away all their clothes and boots to them. They were careful to hide them from the Germans who apparently took many of their personal belongings.

March 16, 1945.

I am listening to an excellent Irish musical program coming from the States. No doubt they are getting the American public ready for the 17th of Ireland. When I was in Dublin, I was told that there was only one other place outside of Ireland that celebrated with proper dignity and propriety, the birth of their Saint, and that was New York. I told them that they better put Toronto on the calendar. In fact, I told them that we celebrated on the 16th as well as the 17th. That really shook them up.

I was informed this evening that I would be going on my leave on Sunday night. Somehow I'm not overly enthusiastic about it. I know it will be nice for me to visit my relatives. Some of the lads who went in the first group returned this evening and they came back feeling like a million. One of the married fellows who hadn't told his wife he was coming, tells me she just about fainted when he came walking through the door. He looked like a new man with a new lease on life.

My mornings seem to be given over to interviews and right now the majority of them are coming from men who wish to get married on their leave to England. My afternoon nap was disturbed by a drunk who just wanted to come in and do a bit of crying on my shoulder. He was just very unhappy with himself and like all drunks, everybody in the world is wrong but himself. I must say that the beer the lads get here is very mild, and I understand you can drink gallons of it without it having any effect. So far I've managed to get along on orangeade and water. While in Italy I took something like 1200 feet of film and today it was returned to me developed. I have been playing around with it all afternoon. It's going to be quite a job to splice it all. Most of it looks pretty decent. It will be something to keep the lads amused when they get back to civilization, when some night they have a party and their families are in attendance. There are a number of good lads on the film who have paid the supreme sacrifice. I know their families would appreciate seeing them just in that way.

March 17, 1945.

"Shure it's a happy Saint Patrick's Day I'm wishing you". The day is perfect. It seems as though the old Saint was around early this morning giving the weatherman his proper instructions. Only the lads of the Irish knew what the day was all about. I had quite a time explaining it to the old lady in the house. The saint who was supposed to be in power around here today was *'dethroned'* and we gave old Paddy a break. I think every company is having a party tonight and all the inhabitants of the local villages are invited. Around here, if you ask one, all the rest come. They just don't feel like letting any member of the family miss anything.

Tonight of course, we had our officers do. I didn't get home from the party until after midnight and since everyone in the house was asleep, I didn't like to go pounding on a typewriter. The party proved to be very good. Nursing sisters from one of our hospitals were our guests. For the first time a lot of what I usually expect, drinking and drunks, was absent. The local town band played the music and did a splendid job. Our pipes filled in for *'Paddy's Road To Dublin'*. As usual it was a bit rough.

This morning I had a couple of church services and as I'm going on leave this afternoon, I had to cut out my afternoon one. In about an hour we are to be visited by General Montgomery. Everyone is on his toes. I'm hoping I can get a few good pictures of him. The day is just about right for it. All I want him to do is stop and talk to some of the lads so I can get a closeup. I understand he likes getting his picture taken so I'm not looking for too much trouble. When the local inhabitants find out that he is coming around, they will go wild. He seems to be a very big favourite with the Belgians. Part of his army gave them their liberation, so he's just one great soldier in their eyes.

So many hours have passed. I do wish the old clock of victory would strike. The advances being made on this front should soon spell the end of the Hun. Already our lads are in a betting mood. The limit is now set anywhere from one month to three. Naturally I'm the fellow who makes it the shortest. It can end tomorrow as far as I'm concerned. I just want to get a-hiking home.

We've Moved to Holland

March 29, 1945.

I just arrived back at the Unit from leave. Since we are now in Holland I was given an extra opportunity of seeing some more country before eventually catching up with them. We are back in the line again but our spirits are very high. Things are very quiet. I guess the Hun is too busy elsewhere to bother too much with us. I just pray he keeps it up. The news every hour is encouraging. We are making rapid progress. It looks as if German resistance is at an end. It's beginning to look like a bit of a chase. If the present progress continues, it may be only a matter of weeks before victory is ours.

While we are still in the line nothing is happening. All we hear is the odd buzz-bomb going over. We have yet to have a casualty of any kind. We are living in very fine houses. The civilians have lost so much. Civilians here are nowhere to be seen In the battle area. This is indeed different from our fronts in Italy.

April 4, 1945.

Since it's far into the night, most of the lads in the R.A.P. have gone off to bed. The M.O. and I challenged a couple of the lads to a game of bridge and it lasted for about three hours. We got well and truly licked, so won't be going about boasting for a day or two. The fact that we can take so much time for cards, is a good indication of how busy we are. The way it is now is the way we like it.

Today I was moving around a nearby battlefield and found a good number of English dead. Consequently I got busy and made a little cemetery for them. They have been dead for sometime so it turned out to be a very gruesome task. Fortunately I was able to identify them which will bring some comfort to their loved ones. Somehow I don't think some of the English chaplains do as careful a job as they should.

We are still getting along very well. I pray good fortune continues to be on our side. The war news is so awfully good and hopeful it would be a shame to see any of our lads get themselves hurt.

April 5, 1945.

Today I kept myself busy picking up enemy dead and seeing to it that they got a decent burial. One can't help but feel the futility of war when you see the end it gives to friend and foe alike. Soon, please God, we will see the end of all this human destruction. Had Germany a proper government, the war would have ended the day we crossed the Rhine.

Here the spring season is well underway. Blossoms and flowers of all descriptions are out in all their glory. The weather is not what one could call ideal. We seem to be getting regular April showers. Of course, it doesn't compare with the rains we got so regularly in Italy, nor does it produce the same kind of mud. Good fortune still continues with us. It's truly the first occasion that I have been happy in action. It begins to look as if the Hun has lost all his fight and confidence. The general picture certainly indicates the fall of all organized resistance. What is making them continue?

April 7, 1945.

Today was just about as perfect as it could be. I used the occasion to visit all the companies. Some of them have very funny positions. Men sure know how to make the best of their surroundings. I found the lads all in good shape and in good spirits and anxious to know when the war is going to finish.

We have a little brush up centre behind the lines where the lads come in small groups for a bath, special meal and a movie. Very few of the lads look tired or unhappy. Most of them have bikes, so they just ride back and forwards to their positions. It all looks like a bit of a picnic. Things are still going very well with us. We heard today that airborne troops had landed ahead of us. That may help to rush this part of the campaign to an end.

There is a large orchard right behind the house we're in. Right now the trees are all out in bloom. Truly it is a glorious sight. At the moment our rations are tops and since we have an excellent cook our food is ideal. In every way we are far ahead of our days in Italy. There is no comparison.

I had a letter from Toronto today indicating that I'll be returning to take over Knox Presbyterian. I really don't know how such rumours start.

April 10, 1945.

I have just been listening to the news of the fall of Hanover and fighting is now taking place in Bremen. On this front tonight, the news is very good. If Monty can keep on going he will soon be shaking hands with the Russians in the North. I'm now just playing the part of the spectator. This afternoon the M.O. and I went down to the rest centre and had a wonderful shower. The lads have the place fixed up very well. After the shower we took in the movie 'The Lady Takes a Chance'. Jean Arthur was the star and the lads thought it quite good.

After supper tonight à couple of the boys and I took a walk. On the way we stopped in to look at some houses. It seems a crime to see lovely furniture, drapes, pictures and children's toys all smashed to pieces. When the owners return they will be heart-broken. Of course, such material things are not to be compared with the tragic loss of human life.

April 13, 1945.

It was a great shock to all of us to hear over the news, of the sudden death of

Roosevelt. Poor man has been under such a heavy strain over these past few years. At a time like this when the President's ideals for freedom and peace are so necessary, it seems untimely that he should be called away at such a critical hour. The foundation for a better world, so well laid by him, will I'm sure, be carried to a successful completion by those who follow in his steps. He was certainly well thought of and today his name and works are upon the lips of every soldier. It is too bad that he didn't live to see the ultimate defeat of Germany. Since Providence makes no mistakes, we must accept such happenings as part of His plan for all of us. Hitler will find little comfort in making much profit from the President's death, since the American troops are now only 60 miles from Berlin.

April 14, 1945.

The lads at this moment are doing a grand job. I never remember so many prisoners being taken by the Unit. All of them are lads around sixteen and seventeen. Some appear to be a bit fanatical ... still have a little of the old '*Hitler bug*' in their systems.

We liberated a town last evening and you should have seen the welcome the people gave us! The Hun thought he would take it back from us at first light this morning. We still have it ... it was a costly try for them. We are fighting through heavy-wooded country and since it is a good spot for the Hun to hide, the lads have developed their own way of digging them out and rounding them up. A few snipers are still in the area and while I was burying a lad today, I was shot at. The lads helping me, went out after him and soon brought him in. He was just a kid but I could have boxed his ears.

The citizens are doing all they can to assist us and do what we call a '*stellar job*'. Things look kind of quiet tonight so maybe we will get some sleep. I haven't had much these past few days.

April 19, 1945.

I'm finding it quite difficult to get letters written. The pace at which we travel, gives us little time. Indeed it is hard enough to arrange for a meal. I often dreamt about a war like this but never thought we would ever experience it. The going was so slow and hard in Italy, we thought it was the way a war should be. Here, however, we go along with the tanks out in front, and when we strike a town or pocket of resistance we stop and clean it up. It may take just a few hours, then off we go again.

As we travel along we go through some of the grandest country and towns. Yesterday you would have thought it was the Twelfth of July. Men, women and little children were all dressed up in orange sashes with bows in their hair. The welcome we are getting is hard to describe. Everybody is out cheering, shaking your hand. I noticed some of the girls kissing the lads. I haven't had that experience yet! I met a good number of Dutch Presbyterian ministers. They seem a fine lot of men. They do a lot of work in Red Cross Centres and open their homes and churches to us. Indeed they are the first people you see when you come to a town. At one town yesterday morning, the minister held a service of thanksgiving outside his ruined church. While I didn't understand the "lingo" I still could feel a very sincere spirit present.

Their underground is excellent. All they want to do is get arms from us. When they get them, they go out and round up the Huns in hiding.

April 20, 1945.

The people in this beautiful Dutch town are in the midst of their celebration of liberty. Our pipe band was on hand to add its colourful roll. The people had never seen a pipe band before and they went crazy over them. While all this fun was going on, the underground lads were bringing in Hun prisoners and collaborators. As they marched them down the main street all the pent up emotions of five years of bondage was let loose. The Dutch gals who were in the Germans' *'good books'* got one of the finest haircuts ... yes, better than some of our criminals. It seems a strange way to take revenge.

Later last night I went over to visit the civilian hospital with the M.O. We visited one ward but that just meant we had to do them all. The patients just wanted to get a close up of their Canadian liberators. As I shook hands with them many just broke down and cried.

This morning I took our pipe band to the hospital and were they ever pleased. The boys put on a real show for them. I think they played every Irish tune ln the book. They gave them a good hour of their time and I knew by the look on their faces it brought a lot of joy to their hearts. It's hard to believe that among so much personal and collective gaiety there is really a tragic war going on. The receptions we are getting certainly lift the morale of the boys. I think they love the fuss.

April 22, 1945.

The war has taken on a very new aspect. No longer do we sit for days up to our knees in mud and take a pounding from the Hun guns. For us, it has become a mad race. It's war on wheels! Yesterday we drove all day without bumping into the enemy. We covered possibly 100 miles. We are now stopped at a very attractive Dutch town. As we entered last night the people came out in droves, giving us a welcome. When they knew we were staying for the night they just got around the men and took them to their homes to sleep. The M.O. and I are staying at the home of a Presbyterian minister. They just gave us the best of what they had. One of the nice things in this country is that everyone can speak a little English. I think some of them speak it better than we do. I can only say that this is the way a war should be fought!

This morning the M.O. and I were surprised when the minister came to our room with tea. Later he brought us hot water to shave. Indeed we are getting spoiled very quickly!

This afternoon I'm holding my service in his church and that will be something very new for us. I know the men will be pleased to worship in a church. We haven't been able to do that since we left England. The band played the troops to the service and there were literally hundreds of people following. When I came to get into the church, it must have taken me five minutes to get through the crowd. The church inside was pretty well like the Presbyterian churches back home, except that the pulpit seemed to be almost up to the roof. We took up a collection for the Dutch Church Restoration Fund and the lads kicked in 308 gilders (about $130.00).

April 24, 1945.

Although we are always on the move, we are moving in the right direction. The news is absolutely wonderful. The Russians seem to be making great headway in Berlin. Seems funny to hear that Hitler is still there. I can hardly believe it. On the west, the gap between ourselves and the Russians is getting smaller and smaller. Possibly by tomorrow it will be closed. The news from Italy is also good. Tonight they are across the Po. Definitely the Hun is finished there.

We are continuing to enjoy our sojourn in Holland. Yesterday for example, before we pulled away for our advance, the minister and his wife gave the M.O. and I a pound of fresh butter. They really know how to make butter in this country. I wish you could travel for a day with us. It does one's heart good to see the Dutch People smile. It's a smile of a liberated people and that's really something!

April 26, 1945.

We have stopped for a breather. Somehow we know that we are quickly coming to the end of this awful business. We learned this morning that the Russians had surrounded Berlin. Now all we want to hear is that they have taken Hitler alive. No matter where you look in our battlefronts, it's the same grand story ... success and progress.

Things are going mighty fine with us. It's difficult to imagine we are really fighting a war. We are getting our share of German prisoners and they seem very happy to be out of it. Of course, the lads have to surround them before they give up. I guess they still have some hope Hitler will even yet do something to rescue them and their lost cause.

We are continuing to find the Dutch people a grand lot to work with. They certainly are out to help us all they can. They have a fine underground. No matter where we go we find them. I think if they were given enough arms, they would finish off the Hun themselves.

April 29, 1945.

Today our worst resistance is coming from the weather. It's rained most of the day and there is a bitter wind blowing; however, we have no kick about the elements here. The lads who suffer most are our poor infantry. I was speaking to some of them this morning and they were wet right up to their 'nicks.' Getting a change of clothes in the line is a bit of a problem so they wear them until they dry out on their bodies. I laughed at one of our lads this morning who was taking back some prisoners. I said, "You look pretty wet." He replied, "Have you looked over my friends?" It's really wonderful how high their spirits are since they have come to this country.

I heard on the six o'clock news that they have murdered Mussolini and his gang. The Italians have certainly taken matters into their own hands. I also heard that Hitler had only a day or so to live. Possibly it would save us a lot of unnecessary trouble if he did die before the Russians got to him. Looks now as if anyday will bring us to the end.

May 2, 1945.

I have been very busy these past few days. I was tired and wet last night when I came in and hadn't any ambition to write. We have been having a lot of rain and when you have to go out in it, especially through fields, you get wet right up to your waist. The evening sky is clearing, so possibly we may get some good weather.

I was listening to the BBC news tonight. Most of it was devoted to the plans for peace day. As it was coming in the Hun was throwing all kinds of shells into our area. Personally I feel they would be better to wait until men have ceased to be wounded and killed before they get excited about peace day celebrations. The war won't be over for us until we kill or capture the Hun we are now fighting.

The War Is Over

May 4, 1945.

Five minutes ago the BBC broke in with the thrilling news that the war in Holland, North-West Germany and Denmark would come to an end tomorrow morning at 8:00 a.m. You should have seen how happy we all were when we got the word. I know it will bring much joy back home. Already we are asking how long it will take us to get home. As far as we are concerned there will be no more battles to fight. I suppose we will have to do a little cleaning up although in this country, I feel the German will be very pleased to get out as fast as he can. The Dutch have no use for the Hun so I think he will run to us for cover as quickly as possible.

For the last few days the Regiment has been on a major drive and everyone was busy. On May 2 we managed to carry out one of the best operations yet. We took about 2000 prisoners ... that will give some indication of the kind of fortifications we were up against. The lads make it so hot for the Hun he was indeed ready to surrender. Bill Elder and his company had the honour of capturing the Commandant of the area. He handed his gun over to Bill and asked for protection for his men. We were kind of busy in the R.A.P. (mostly German wounded) so I didn't get up to the town till the morning was nearly over. I did manage to get a few movies of what was left, along with a very good German car. I think it belonged to one of the "bigshots". It's now in my service and doing an excellent job. I don't know how long I can keep it; all I know is that it's just ideal for my job so am hoping it will be with me until my work in this part of the world is completed.

On May 3, we had the situation well in hand, so I spent the day doing a little of my own work. I'm glad it didn't amount to what was expected. Around 1:00 p.m. we were taken out of the line and brought back to a rear area where the lads are getting cleaned up. The weather has been very bad, so we are all up to our necks in mud. Of course, we don't mind it for we've seen something very big for our efforts.

Today I visited the local minister and made arrangements to use his church on Sunday. He speaks English so very well, it was a most pleasant visit. He had some very unpleasant experiences with the Germans, and is much overjoyed that we have come. Now that we have gotten the good news, our service on Sunday will be one of thanksgiving. The only regret I have at this moment are the lads we have lost during our battles in Holland. Amid all the joy that must be going on in Canada tonight, there are many who will be most sad. It will be difficult for them to find an answer to the loss of their loved ones, now that the end has come for us in this country. What a blessed day when there will be no more death to report; no more next-of-kin letters to write; no more wounded to evacuate. One can only thank God for His wonderful mercy, care and protection. I'm sure He has answered our prayers and we have much to be thankful for. I can only pray that my homecoming won't be withheld too long.

May 6, 1945.

It's difficult for us to believe that the end has finally come. Somehow there is stillness around our dwelling that is most uncanny. It's now thirty hours since we last heard the sound of a gun and just as many hours since we attended to our last casualty. The last one we worked on in the field was a German. Tonight we are resting in a very small Dutch village. It has had some excitement since the news of the liberation has come. Everywhere their national flag was flying. Young and old were decked out in their national colour – orange.

The question that troubles us most is where do we go from here? How long will it take the government to get us back home? Naturally, each one feels that all that remains is to get us on boats and headed out to sea. I don't think it will be quite as easy as that. I personally feel that we may have to do a spot of occupational duty in Germany. While this may appear to be a bit of hardship, still I'm so happy to get out of this business alive. I'll only regard a bit of extra time as a rotten inconvenience. It's a great day and one of personal joy to know that I will be coming home. I can say now that there were days and nights when I often wondered if I would make the grade. I know I owe so much to God for his daily and constant care. I can honestly say that He has seen me safely through and I only hope I may in the days that are before me, remain true and faithful to Him.

I see that they eventually found out at home that I won the M.C. The C.O. arranged a mess dinner and ordered all the officers to dress. When I got to the mess Sunday evening I felt like a fish out of water — I came in my dirty battle dress. Nothing was said till dinner was about to begin, then Leigh called everyone into the mess and said he had a pleasant duty to perform. He made a nice speech and walked over and pinned the M.C. on me. I was quite shocked. I really didn't know what to say. I feel after the fine work of some of our officers here in Holland, that some of them ought to be getting a few decorations. How some of them didn't is beyond me, particularly for their work in Italy. A good number were recommended. So far I haven't seen the citation so don't know how I came to get it. All the C.O. would tell me was it was for something I did in action. Decorations in war should go to the wives and mothers who, as far as I am concerned, are the real heroes.

This morning I held a service in a very attractive Dutch church. I preached from Joshua 22. I spoke about the dangers of victory. This period for the average soldier is going to be a difficult one. The church was badly damaged by shell fire, so the Irish lads came through again with a fine donation of $200.00 as their gift for the restoration work. It's nice to know that our lads care.

May 8, 1945.

At long last we have come to the end of the war. Now that it's actually here it's really quite hard to believe. It has been a long struggle and now that we are the victors, it's really a bit difficult to know how to act. Today we were given the day off. The little Dutch town where we are staying is all aflame with the news. One can't go out on the street without having old and young give you the right kind of greeting. Last night I noticed the girls were going for our lads in a big way. Leave it to the Canadian boys to know how to act under such conditions. Tonight at one minute after midnight, we will officially celebrate the victory. Many things have been organized for the event. It will likely turn out like a 24th of May celebration. To bring our festivities to a close we are having one great bonfire. 'Hitler and Mussolini' will go into the fire to the tune of the pipes. The local citizens are doing their bit, so all in all if we don't fall off to sleep, it should be a pretty good show.

I heard Mr. Churchill's speech this afternoon. I didn't think he was in his best form. I expected he would praise the Empire to the skies and in doing so would take the opportunity to tell the Germans some pressing truths. All that was absent. Being a good Englishman, I suppose he was adhering to the sporting instinct of not kicking a man when he is down. In about an hour the King will be on the air and I feel he will have something worthwhile to say. He appears to have such a sincere approach to the whole matter. He always leaves a good impression when he speaks. This is really one day that all serving men should be with their loved ones back home to experience the real emotion that has been pent up these five years.

May 9, 1945.

I personally thought that with Victory Day would come a problem of over celebrating in our army ranks. As a matter of fact, it has turned out to be the opposite. I don't think the lads fully realize what has happened. Last night when we had our do, the thing that struck me most was how little the men actually entered into it. The local citizens were having a whale of a time. They dressed their little town all up in lights and gay colours. They followed the pipe band with great mirth, as it paraded down their streets. They cheered to high heaven at the bonfire when it was lit, especially when the pipes played the '*Wearin' of the Green*' as Hitler and Mussolini, dressed for the burning, went up in smoke. While this was going on our lads were just good spectators. They showed no signs of emotion. Somehow it didn't seem to be their day. Our hearts and minds are turned homeward, where we know those who love us were really going out on our behalf. I believe that all of us know our day for victory will really come when once again we sight the shores of Canada and look into the faces of those whom we call our very own. This morning, I dressed up in my Irish togs and headed for the mess where the C.O. had a special dinner laid on for all his officers. It was a real '*humdinger*'. We had about seven courses and here again our get together was marked by sobriety.

This afternoon I took a drive in my little German car, to have a last look at our battlefield. It was strangely silent, yet there was much evidence around to remind one that a war had passed this way. I noticed people had come back to their homes. Here and there, from the top of a ruined home, where they were making repairs, they took time out to wave and shout a great big hello. The farmers, too, were busy in their fields and men were repairing broken bridges and roads. How gallant a lot of people these Dutch are. Many of the Italians were satisfied to sit in the ruins, but the Dutch make haste in removing the scars of war.

May 11, 1945.

The weather we are having these past few days is quite in keeping with the excellent news our world is now enjoying. So far the Dutchman hasn't stopped celebrating. Indeed, he seems more excited about the end of hostilities than we poor soldiers do.

Ours is a strange world. There's such a silence and stillness among our ranks it's almost unbelievable. Our task now is to keep the minds of the men occupied. They put in their mornings doing P.T. drilling and route marches. The afternoon is all theirs and we are doing all we can to organize sports, trips and shows to fill up their time.

Yesterday I gave the whole day to my next-of-kin letters. I had 21 to write. That is the total of our fatal casualties since coming to Holland. It is a tragedy, with the war in its last stages, to have lost so many fine lads. So far none of the lads have died of wounds and it now looks as if we may have a perfect score in that direction. I understand that next week we will know if we are to be involved in occupational duty.

May 17, 1945.

Bill is now in the possession of a very good Jerry car, so we used it to drive down. The day was perfect for the trip. Since the Dutch are still celebrating, we were given a rousing welcome as we drove through their towns and villages. Some of their decorations are absolutely unique. We got to Otterloo around five and went to the local minister's home, where he set up a place for us to sleep. When the locals heard the Irish were in town, it wasn't long till we had visits from a good number of them. On Tuesday morning I filmed the high spots of our battle there. The cemetery where I buried five of our lads is in grand order. All the graves had flowers on them.

At 5:00 p.m. a committee of the town of Otterloo met and invited Bill and I to be present. They presented the Regiment with a Dutch Bible, two pictures and clogs. Yesterday morning the Queen of the Otterloo underground made a presentation to Bill of a walking stick. She is a very attractive girl. At the conclusion of the ceremony she gave Bill a kiss — was he ever taken back! Since I have it recorded on film we have it for posterity.

May 18, 1945.

Yesterday I conducted a funeral service for one of our lads who fell off a truck the night before and was fatally injured. He was just 21 and a fine lad at that. Now that the war is over it's a most tragic happening. I'm sure his poor family, who live in Sudbury, will be broken hearted.

I attended a concert last evening put on by an English company. It was very well done and the talent the best I have seen in an army show for a long time. We are doing very well with entertainment right now. I guess the army authorities feel they have to keep our evenings full. So far our lads have been no trouble. The C.O. of course, is making life very pleasant for them. Every-day there are trips somewhere and every night trucks take them into the city of Groningen, where there seems to be a lot going on.

I heard from home and apparently 75 returned Irish lads attended York Church. I thought that was a very fitting gesture and makes me feel very proud. The lads hadn't forgotten their old padre. This afternoon we had a chaplains' meeting in Groningen. As chaplains we're soon to start an extensive educational program among the troops. I suppose they feel they want to keep us busy too.

I imagine everyone at home is getting ready for the coming Provincial and Federal elections. Already I have received some circulars from candidates. All seem to have an excellent program on paper for the returning soldier. I guess the day of political promises will never end. I haven't quite made up my mind who I will vote for. While I haven't any sympathy for the King regime over the war years, I don't see much opposition to prevent his administration from taking office again.

This morning I gave over to official correspondence and this afternoon I took one of our lads to the cemetery to see his brother's grave. Strange he was away on leave to England when his brother was killed. We have had very poor luck with brother combinations in the Regiment. Some nine have been killed.

One of the lads going on leave to England wanted to take a new bonnet to another of our lads in hospital there. After I got him the bonnet he said "Padre, I think you must own this Regiment, for I tried all the 'high-priced' help and none of them could get it for me." He is a very nice lad who always goes around with a smile on his face.

The Waiting Game

May 26, 1945.

I recall it was just a year ago today that I miraculously missed being killed. When I picked up the broken bodies of the lads who were riding with me in the jeep, I couldn't help but feel many prayers on my behalf were being answered. That night, even though I was sleeping out on the damp ground of Italy and the shells were coming in thick and fast, my thoughts of home and family kept me going till the break of day. Since we still don't know when our homecoming is going to get underway, we are all hoping that it won't take too long. There is precious little going on in the Regiment these days. A couple of companies are away in the west of Holland escorting German prisoners back to Germany. I keep myself busy with '*Padre's Hour*' and for some reason I'm beset with personal interviews. I'm really having some funny ones. One of the lads, married to a girl in England, received a letter from his wife that she was going to have a baby and couldn't understand it, except perhaps, because she slept in his pajamas! The lad is looking for a divorce.

Last night we played a Dutch team and beat them 3-1. I scored two goals.

May 27, 1945.

The electricity has just been turned on in our little town. It adds greatly to our personal comfort. Since we don't have to worry about blackouts, we just turn on the juice everytime we see a light switch. All these little things will break us in for the comfort and peace of our own homes.

Today I held a service in the local church, followed by communion. The lads do appreciate services on a voluntary basis. This afternoon our Division opened a Chaplains' House in Groningen. It was really a wonderful gathering with a grand supper that added to the event. This week three day Bible courses were started. We are allowed four men a week. I have to go in and take my turn at teaching which I'm ill prepared for.

May 29, 1945.

I understand some 15,000 officers and men are going home this month. Among them will be the volunteers for the East. This afternoon my educational corporal got his '*go*' papers. He is leaving May 31. He has been overseas 3½ years with about 204 points. I have 174 so possibly it won't take them too long to get to me.

Yesterday I put in my morning at our weekly chaplain meeting. All of us had dinner together in our newly opened Chaplains' House. Our senior chaplain is also returning to Canada next month. He has been overseas since December 1939. As long as we know Canadian personnel are on the move home, it helps the rest of us awaiting our turn.

We have started a six-week religious instruction course within the Division. I have seven hours a week with the Unit. The course is very interesting, although I wish the men could have an opportunity to do some solid reading on it. The outline of the courses is 'The Soldier and His God, Home, Country.' I had my first session this morning. I took three companies, spending an hour with each.

This afternoon word came down that we are to move into Groningen. I think we will get in there on Thursday. I would just as soon remain here, but the lads will be closer to entertainment, so that should make them a little happier.

May 31, 1945.

Men with over 200 points left the Regiment this morning on their way home to Canada. Bob Butler was all smiles as he bid me goodbye. He's been working with me so long I'm going to miss his assistance very much.

Last night in one of the Groningen hotels our Brigadier gave a dance for all the officers in the Brigade. George Duncan and I went in. The place was very crowded. I had one dance with a Dutch lassie, ate a couple of sandwiches, jumped into the car and came home again. I'm afraid I'm not very sociable when I'm thinking of getting home. Our General was there. Earlier in the afternoon he had learned he was appointed to command the Pacific force. In a little speech he made, he said our 5th Division men that wanted to come with him would be assured a spot. I didn't hear that one! I'm silent on that theatre of operation.

June 5, 1945.

I must say that these are very difficult days to put in. I find the old spirit of restlessness growing each day. I have but one thought and it governs all I try to do.

Yesterday the General came to say goodbye to the Regiment. He left today for Canada where he will form his staff and get ready for the East. We expect Leigh Payne to leave on Friday.

We held a mess dinner last evening in honour of Leigh. It was the best we ever had. I don't know when any of us had more fun. Our doings lasted till the wee hours. I guess we're just a lot of boys at heart and foolish ones at that.

Tomorrow morning our first draft from the Regiment leaves for the East by way of Canada. There will be about 75 in it. Altogether we have had about 250 volunteers. That is the largest of any Regiment over here. Paul LaPrairie who is also going is in charge of them.

June 7, 1945.

I spent the day at our Divisional Chaplains' school. I started in with a half hour of devotions. Next I gave them an hour on the Book of Colossians. We had a half-hour break and then another hour on the *'Faith of the Church'*. My particular subject was *'Redemption.'* From the mess lecture we went to the mess hall and had dinner together. The afternoon up until 4:30 p.m., was given to sight-seeing around the city of Groningen. After we returned I gave another lecture on the *'Work of the Church Today.'* While I feel pretty tired this evening, still, I don't know when I enjoyed doing anything more than this job. I found the men most receptive and vitally interested in the topics.

Yesterday the first draft for the East, left the Unit. The boys were really excited. I had a little chat with them before they pulled away and some of them said "Padre, you should be coming with us." Of course, to such remarks I have but one answer. Another draft leaves tomorrow. At this rate we soon won't have a Regiment left.

According to our papers today, I see Ontario elected the Conservatives. I really thought that the c.c.f. would have made more ground, instead of losing it. I'm glad to see that the party in got a good working majority. They surely can do things now.

June 11, 1945.

No doubt political aspirations will be running high in Canada today. The accounts we get of political battles leading up to the election, sounds as if Canada is taking the election seriously. Since the next five years are going to be very important, I only hope whoever does get in will get a working majority. I tend to despair when I read the *'Utopia'* some of the parties are advocating. The most the average soldier wants is the opportunity to make a decent living.

This morning at eight we said goodbye to our Commanding Officer. Leigh Payne really took his departure quite hard. As he went around shaking hands with the officers and men, he just couldn't keep back the tears. I almost felt like shedding a few myself. He flies first to England and from there to Canada. Our 5th Anniversary supper dance turned out very well. I got on my way at 8:00 p.m. but called it an evening around midnight. The Dutch lassies did a fine job of entertaining the gang. I think our food at the dinner just about knocked them over. They hadn't seen so much in many a year. I thought they would never finish. Since I didn't have a girl, I assisted in passing out the food. It was just like throwing biscuits to a bear!

The country at present looks very nice. The people are busy painting their homes and cleaning up the last bit of war damage. This city got off very lightly so they won't be too long getting back Into their usual routine. Their farms appear in excellent shape, and it looks as if North Holland will have a bumper harvest.

June 16, 1945.

Yesterday we spent most of the day moving from Groningen to Heerenveen. The citizens of Groningen were out in the hundreds to bid us goodbye. We arrived in Heerenveen late in the afternoon. Our first job was getting ourselves located. I was most fortunate in my set up. My sleeping quarters are in a private home. I have a most splendid bedroom with twin beds, running water and a basin right in the room. Next to my bedroom, is a very excellent furnished sitting room, and this too has been given by the lady of the house for my private use. Indeed, I'm twice blessed, for downstairs I have my office. It compares very favourably with the kind of thing our stock exchange lads use on Bay St. I thought my Groningen set up couldn't be surpassed, but this has it outstripped in a good many ways.

The town itself is most attractive. Like most Dutch towns it's the very essence of cleanliness. All the local centres of entertainment have been turned over for our private use. This morning the local minister and I got the full use of his church for our Sunday services. The whole Regiment is not here. 'B' and 'C' companies are located at a town about four miles away. We stopped there for a few days during our fighting period, so the place is well known to our men. There again the troops are well looked after, so be it a long or short period, we are at least going to enjoy our surroundings.

We are still waiting to hear something definite on our move home. We did hear the Canadian forces would be returning by divisions and this is the way they have it drawn up: First Division (August); Second Division (September); Third Division (October); Fifth Division (November); Fourth Division, the last to come over, (December). It is thought that since our points are high, we may be moved up with the Second and Third Divisions and come home with them. This order is likely to change tomorrow so what's the use of making any plans.

June 18, 1945.

Yesterday I went to Joure and held services for 'B' and 'C' companies. I remained for dinner with Bill Elder. The companies there have very pleasant surroundings and since the men are all in private billets, they usually have the household along with them when they go anywhere. It is just like old home week when the lads have a parade or a move.

This morning I left for Groningen to attend a chaplains' meeting. We learned who were the chaplains going to the East and to occupational duty. My name, of course, was not on the list. Most of the men going have not had the service of some of us. We gave them our blessing. We hoped to hear something definite on our return to Canada. So far those in authority are in a muddle. I was saying to the boss-chaplain, that if they don't soon hurry, I will make my own private arrangements. One gets awfully tired of the waiting around.

I!m getting a real kick out of my 'Padre's Hour.' The men agree that unfaithfulness was the greatest threat to home life today, but also agreed there was more unfaithfulness among the average Canadian married soldier, than there was among the average Canadian wife. Some of them had the strangest way of expressing their ideas.

June 19, 1945.

The heat is so intense these days one would almost think we were back home enjoying our good Canadian summer. Unlike Italy, no provision is made for the wearing of summer drill; consequently we are suffering under the burden of our battle dress. It got a little too much for me yesterday, so I pulled out my own summer stuff and put it on. You should have been in the mess when I walked in with it. Did I ever take a going over. However, at suppertime most of my fellow officers had followed my example.

There's real excitement around the Regiment today. Some 50 men with 174 points got their call for a Canadian draft. We never thought it would happen, since men with 200 points were the only ones that were being called. We have some 250 men in the 170 point range, myself included. I am, however, considered a 'key man' so may have to remain a little longer. I met all the lads who are going this afternoon to bid them goodbye and so help me I think we are a lot of babies. I guess five years together does something to men. It's at this juncture that I'm very happy to have been able to remain with the Regiment through its active history. Naturally I'm keeping my fingers crossed. It would be wonderful if I could get home on one of these 'Repat drafts'. Since most of the old boys will soon be cleared out, I haven't much desire to stay around and look after those who are coming to replace them.

June 22, 1945.

Another Canadian draft was called this morning and on the list was none other than my faithful batman Ted Reeves. When he heard he was going he came to me and said "If you want me to stay I won't go". I would no more think of keeping him from going than I would myself. He's been packing all day and in between chores has been showing a Dutchman how to become a batman. Men are getting so scarce around the Regiment you have to get someone from anywhere to work for you.

Last evening I took our pipe band over to the local hospital. The staff and patients thoroughly enjoyed it. The hospital staff arranged them so that all could see the band. Later I took in a Dutch stage show, 'Rainbow Review.' It was quite the best I have seen since I left Canada. Many acts were better done than the ones we see coming out of Hollywood. Had I the cash and the inclination, I'd make a fortune with the group. Since most of them spoke and sang their songs in English, it was quite easy to follow.

We are still suffering from an intense heat wave. They have never known the likes of it before in Holland.

June 24, 1945.

This is another beautiful day. This morning I held services in the local Dutch Reformed Church for the companies in Heerenveen. The minister in a very brief yet inspiring message, welcomed us to his church. The Canadians are held in very high regard among all Dutch folk. The troops occupied the lower part of the church and civilians filled the gallery. Since many of them spoke and understood English, they entered right into the service with us. They have requested to be allowed to attend all our church services. Naturally it's all right by us and if anything, adds to our service. It's nice to have female voices singing our hymns.

Saturday Ted, along with 30 other lads, left for Canada. I was really sorry to see Ted leave. He was more than my batman, he was my good friend. In action, when he thought I was taking chances, he used to say, "Always remember, Padre, you have a wife and son." That was always enough.

June 26, 1945.

There is really nothing going on except the usual routine. I only wish they would hurry up and get me home. While I'm very busy, I'm still awfully fed up. Everyday a draft leaves for Canada and since most of them going are old boys, I get kind of lonely when I see them go off. Somehow at this stage being a Padre is not so very hot. We seem to be people they can't get along without.

The Princess Light Field have been added to my spiritual care. With formations being broken up with each becoming smaller everyday, the work of the chaplains here increases, since we must take up the duties of those padres who have already left on draft for Canada.

This afternoon was given to football. I am still trying to keep young. Of course I'm not so very old ... just a wee bit grey.

We heard over the news that so many troops are now coming into Halifax that the C.N. and C.P.R. are unable to handle them. I am sure if they got me as far as Halifax, I could get the rest of the way myself.

I have been busy getting my memorial service and honour roll off to the next-of-kin. Our total count of fatal casualties is 210. I sent copies to all of the families.

June 30, 1945.

Here it is Saturday night and the last night of June. Since tomorrow is a very special day, I decided to stay in and get myself ready. All day menbers of the Irish scattered over north-west Europe have been coming im so that they may be on hand for the service. Some have been away from us since our early days in Italy, so naturally we are having a bit of a reunion. It's raining quite hard tonight. I only hope we are favoured with a good bright day tomorrow.

I have just listened to the Canadian news and heard some 8000 troops arrived this week in Halifax. It will take a long time to get us home if that's the best they can do. I am still hopeful that my name will appear on one of the drafts. I understand that they are trying to work on a system whereby chaplains like myself, with high points, will get away like any other officer or man when his name shows up on the draft list. You can be sure that I'll be in there pulling for D.P.R. Sometimes I feel like I would like to go back and put the top on York Church. From here that looks like a lot of very hard work.

July 1, 1945.

This has turned out to be a very big day for the Irish. The weatherman was on our side making camera work just about perfect. The memorial part of our service, got underway at 10:30 a.m. As usual we had the whole town as spectators. Everything clicked as planned even to the lowering and raising of the flag. At the conclusion of this part of the service we marched off to our respective churches. I followed through with the order of service as printed. The troops filled to overflowlng the main body of the church and the civilians packed the gallery. Indeed they were literally sitting on top of each other. At the conclusion of the service, the Protestant and Catholics reformed for the march past, which was done in the best Irish tradition. The men and officers were highly pleased with the service. I don't know when I ever received more compliments for a piece of work done. I had 3000 printed and now I find I won't have enough. The demand for copies goes beyond my expectations.

After dinner I drove to Groningen where I attended our chaplains' meeting. While there I learned that high point chaplains would be repatriated. I find I'm among the lucky ones and just before I commenced this letter I sent off the necessary particulars on myself to the chief chaplain. There is only one other chaplain with more points than I in the Division and he is going to the East, so I believe I have a very good chance of making the grade.

July 2, 1945.

I received a message today telling me I was to report at Buckingham Palace, June 13, to receive my M.C. from the King. Further details are to follow. I am certainly excited about it. I'm meeting with the King for the second time and count myself quite lucky.

We opened a rest centre at the town of Leeuwarden this morning. George Macartney and I did the honours. It is an excellent spot and I'm sure the men will enjoy it. Fifty men go every three days. I'm thinking of taking in a few days myself. There is an excellent swimming pool that I'd like to spend some time in.

July 4, 1945.

Yesterday I had a very full day. I topped it off with a football game against a crack Dutch squad, which proved far too good for our lads left in the Regiment who can play the game. We got licked 6-0. We had a lot of fun, but I find it a little too much of an effort without enough team support.

I was busy all morning with 'Padre's Hour.' At the moment I'm dealing with the 'Soldier and His Country and His Place in It.' One of the 'Zombies' made the remark that England expects everyone else to fight her battles. The comment angered me so, I asked him how much fighting he had done. I suppose I should be more generous but I can't help but think of some of our lads who might still be alive if they had a little extra help.

This afternoon the General called all the officers to a meeting. He told us that because of the scarcity of shipping, it was not felt that the 5th Division would be home in Canada before Easter. That was a bitter pill to awallow after having such a rosy picture painted by those in authority only a few weeks ago. Just seems the Canadian Army has no direction. I fail to see how we cannot get more than a couple of troop ships for our use, particularly when one thinks of the shipping we provided during the war for war materials. My points may even yet save me from such a fate. Our government certainly needs to waken up and give a little more attention to the needs of our soldiers, or else we are going to have a lot of men when they do return, despising the land they so willingly fought for. There is, however, this provision: all men with 150 points, except key personnel, will be sent home. I hope I'm not considered essential. As I often said, leave it to the army to spoil the best laid plans.

July 6, 1945.

Just a little while ago I got word on my trip to England. I'm leaving early Sunday morning. I go by car to Nijmegen and from there to England by plane. The investiture takes place Friday morning, July 13, at 11:00 a.m. I'm permitted to bring two guests, so I thought I would invite my uncle and aunt from Oxford.

Starting Sunday we are having another large Canadian draft leaving the Regiment. After this one goes, the Irish, except for a few key People, will exist in name only. Right now I have some difficulty recognizing who's who! I'll be happy when I manage to hit one of these drafts. Personally my interest under present conditions is waning and it would be best to get me on my way.

We have heard of the impatience of some of the lads in Aldershot, England. I was just afraid something like that would happen. I only hope more shipping space can be found, or else we may have more difficulty. The Canadian soldier is a pretty hard kind of fellow to be made to sit around.

July 7, 1945.

Tomorrow morning I leave for England. I have been busy today getting all fixed up. I guess I, too, have to look as smart as I can when I come up in front of the King.

More excitement would be mine if I were getting ready to return home. Two drafts which were to go tomorrow were cancelled this morning. You should have seen the looks on the faces of tne lads who were affected. They were extremely disappointed. I do wish the government would get busy at something definite. I know that nothing can be achieved by rioting, still it's very hard on the lads. Possibly the next few weeks should make the picture a little clearer.

I had a rush today on Dutch-Canadian marriages. The lads are falling for some of the Dutch girls in a big way. As a matter of fact the Dutch girls impress me very much with their sensible outlook. Before a lad gets permission to marry a Dutch girl, he must wait for a period of four months ... a wise precaution.

The Investiture

July 9, 1945.

I am writing this letter as the ship very slowly pushes its way across the channel. The day is extremely hot and there seems to be little relief coming from the water. The channel is as smooth as silk. You can hardly feel yourself moving along.

I left Heerenveen yesterday morning at ten. Before I got away the batmen went to work on me. They did such a good job dressing me that they had to take a snap before I left, just to prove it. If it comes out, I'll be sending it home. I took a lot of ribbing before I did get away. The drive from Heerenveen to Nijmegen was without incident. I got in at 3:00 p.m. and reported to the officer in charge of the investiture party. He gave me a few drill instructions and told me the party was not flying. That made me angry for we were told we would be.

Just as I was sitting down for supper, in came Crawford Smith. He was beating his gums, for he was told the same story. At seven we were taken by truck to the station where we got on board a train that must have been built around 1900! We rode the thing for eight hours. I just couldn't sleep, it was too uncomfortable. We eventually got into Ostend at 5:00 a.m. We were pretty tired and hungry and made for the mess just as soon as we hit the staging camp. Nothing was known of our arrival here, so began a real army guessing game. First we were going, then we were not. There was a lot of hot talk. Nobody knew anything. At 1:00 a.m. they got us on a boat for Dover. As I said earlier, that is as far as we have gone. We are suppose to land at 7:30 a.m. When our Canadian officials start arranging things they sure make a mess of it. Our trip which should have been a pleasure, has now turned into one big flop.

July 11, 1945.

Yesterday our party arrived in London. We are now on our own till Friday morning, when we meet again at Buckingham Palace.

Our investiture party was so poorly organized, that everybody was ready to quit and forget the whole thing. I'd like to meet the Joe who plans these things! Yesterday Crawford and I broke away from the party at Dover. When the officer in charge wasn't looking, we jumped on a civilian train for London. As it turned out it was well we did, for we learned the party on reaching London, was dispersed till Friday morning!

We got a very nice hotel and everything is designed for our personal comfort, and we are taking full advantage of it. We went out this morning to do a little shopping. Somethings are still pretty difficult to secure. We walked the streets of London and thought how wonderful it would be if we were walking the streets of Toronto.

July 13, 1945.

We went to the Palace by taxi. All London seemed to be crowded around the gates as we drove in. On arriving at the main steps of the Palace door, a very smart policeman guided us into an elegant room. Here our names were checked and we were ushered into our proper place in the line. We waited in this room for about 45 minutes and right on the dot of 11:00 a.m. our line started to move.

While the line was moving, a band played very softly as one by one, we went forward to receive our medals from the King. Eventually my name was called. I went forward, turned left facing the King, bowed, took one step forward and there I was right in front of him. His first words to me after pinning on the Cross were, "Where have I met you before?" I replied, "Sandringham, sir three years ago." "Oh", he said "how did the pictures turn out?" "You were excellent, your majesty" I replied. He asked me a few questions about the Regiment, when I expected to go home, etc. I was amazed he remembered me. I had the distinction out of everyone in attendance, to have had the longest chat with him. When I got outside, many people, whom I didn't even know, were asking me why he talked to me so long and what he had to say. My uncle and aunt were thrilled with all they saw. There were a good number of pictures taken, so I may be sending some home very soon.

July 14, 1945.

My investiture leave is almost over. In a couple of hours I take the train from Victoria Station for Dover, where I will get the boat in the morning for France. I expect the trip back won't be quite as disorganized as the one coming over.

I have remained in London for most of my leave. This is certainly a very crowded city. One gets awfully tired of being jostled and bumPed. Most of the lights are on again, so it's not too difficult to find your way around. I really haven't done anything special on this trip. I took in a couple of movies and one stage show. I also visited a few of our Canadian clubs. I met a few of the fellows I haven't seen for a long time.

July 15, 1945.

I am writing this letter from transit camp 'E' Calais. At the moment we are having a real Canadian electrical storm. The rain is coming down in buckets. Last night I got away from Victoria Station at 11:15 p.m. The crowds were terrific. It almost seemed every soldier had a gal along with him to swell the gathering. Some of the lads have very little decorum. Necking on the platform is as common as chickens on a farm! There doesn't seem to be any modesty left. Maybe I see things just a wee bit differently. The "glad gals" are just as numerous as ever. One can't walk along some of London's streets without being held up. One said to me "Would you like a pleasant evening at the right price?" I replied, "I'm going to have one; I'm on my way to meet my wife." That stopped her dead.

I got into Folkestone around 2:00 a.m. From there we were taken to our rooms. I had a couple of English officers as roommates. They were half shot so you can guess the fun I had listening to their line. One of them was telling the other about the wonderful leave he had with his wife. I was thinking, had his wife heard the stuff he divulged, she would gladly have broken his neck!

I got up at 8:45 this morning. Since the clocks went back an hour, I got an extra hour's sleep. After breakfast we were taken by truck to the ship. The day was perfect, hence the trip across the channel to Calais was just what the doctor ordered. The White Cliffs of Dover stood out in all their loveliness as we sailed by them. A couple of hours sailing, we were on French soil. Much of the French coast is badly damaged. The Hun had some very heavy defenses around that area. Our airforce didn't seem to miss any of them. My train doesn't leave until 10:00 p.m. so I won't be in Nijmegen until tomorrow morning. It's such a long trip, although it's been laid on so well on the return leg, that I won't mind it.

Orders for Home

July 17, 1945.

I returned to the Regiment last night and got my first good news. There was the message from army H.Q.: "You are now available for repatriation and will proceed on Canada draft #224 for Military District #218, Toronto. Your replacement is appointed and you are free to go when your draft number appears in Orders." How long I will have to wait is anyone's guess ... so many rotten things happen in the army. I'm almost afraid to anticipate, just in case. In the meantime, I'm packing so when my movement order comes I'll be out in a flash. I hope to be home by the beginning of September.

July 19, 1945.

At long last my movement orders have come through. My name appeared this morning on draft #224 which instructs me to report to Nijmegen on Monday, July 23, for '*report*' to Canada. I'm so excited I can hardly hold this pen in my hand. It's hard to believe after a long wait that I'll be coming home.

I understand it takes from four to six weeks after you get started before you can expect to see the shores of Canada, which means I will definitely be home for September. There appears to be quite a long wait over in England, and if that is the case and they grant leaves, I will run over and have one more look at Ireland. Naturally I'm now trying to get my gear together. It's quite the job. Really, I'm finding it a bit difficult to contain myself. I only pray nothing happens to prevent my getting away.

I have just been walking around on air. It's a grand feeling even though it is still hard to believe. This is really the day I've been waiting for. There were times I thought it would never come!

July 22, 1945.

I can hardly believe it. I'm on the first leg of my journey. This morning at 10:30 to the tune of the bagpipes, I said my farewells to the officers and men of the Irish Regiment. While there were only a few old officers on hand, it was still hard to leave them behind. I tried to concole them by saying I'd see them before Christmas. The day was in keeping with the wonderful event. The sun just made every bit of the Dutch landscape look so good. I guess I was being left with the best possible morning.

I got to the report camp about three. Everything is well organized here and it doesn't take too long to get your documentation done. I have no idea how long I'll have to stay here. I was speaking to an officer I know on the staff, and he said if everything went well I should be heading for England on Wednesday. One of the highlights here is to receive all the ribbons you're entitled to. I have six coming.

July 25, 1945.

This wlll be my last letter from Holland. In a couple of hours we entrain for Ostend where we get our ship for England. We won!t be in Ostend till 5:00 a.m., which means, as it was in the case of the investiture trip, a most tiresome and uncomfortable journey. This is one trip that nothing can spoil. I'm prepared to ride anything as long as it is taking me in the direction of home. The weather has been ideal since coming here and if it continues it should add to our trip.

July 29, 1945.

I got to England on Thursday night, after a pleasant boat trip. On arrival at Dover, we had our dinner and boarded the trail for a place called Oxshott. Trucks took us from the station to the camp and here we found excellent accommodation.

Friday morning at 9:00 a.m. we had our first parade. The C.O. of the camp called us all together and the first thing he said was, "I'm sorry but you won't be getting your customary leave." We didn't know what was coming off. Then he went on, "You are leaving for Canada sooner than planned." I think the people in London must have heard our cheers. "I'm giving you all five days leave, but you must be back Saturday, August 4." "You will be sailing for Canada on the 8th or 10th of August." We were also told that we would have to go directly to the military district of our original draft, which for me, means Toronto rather than Halifax. If everything goes to plan I should be home by the 20th of August.

August 1, 1945.

Yesterday I spent the day around the camp mess which is located in a very attractive English home. I have everything packed so am ready for my trip home. There has been no change so far in our sailing date. It remains August 8th. We still don't know the ship we are travelling on but, I don't care as long as it gets me home in a hurry. It's just as well that we have to stay with our draft to our final destination. I find I can't tell anyone the name of the post where we come in. It may be Quebec, Montreal, Halifax or New York. Personally I hope it is New York. It would be a terrible trick if we got mixed up in our meeting plans.

I came up to London this morning. I am only twenty minutes away by train. I'm having my bank account transferred over. I have managed to save a few dollars.

These are pretty exciting days for me. I can hardly eat or sleep and when I do I have my family in my dreams.

August 6, 1945.

This is my last letter from this side of the world. We leave tomorrow night for the ship. So far we have not been told from what port we sail, or on what ship. Neither have we been told at what port in Canada we expect to arrive. If we sail on the 8th, and that is now our target date, we should be in Toronto between the 15th and 20th. I would think our arrival will be closer to the 15th than any other date.

It's been a very long wait and now that it's within reach, I find myself as excited as I can be.

August 9, 1945.

Just as we were all ready to pull out for the ship, it was called off! Our target date is now August 12th.

It's just one of those things one can do nothing about. I am just sitting tight, hoping and praying we won't be disappointed again. I guess you can't really count on being away until you are actually on the ship and heading towards Canada.

Yesterday I jumped on the train and went to visit Colonel Clark, now a full Colonel. He was delighted to see me and I certainly had a grand time visiting with him. He gave me the use of his staff car and driver for the afternoon. I drove around to see a few places that I knew and returned to our quarters at 7:00 p.m.

Today, I'm orderly officer which keeps me close to the camp. A good number of men are here, so one has to get them on parade by 9:00 a.m., inspect their quarters and make out daily leave passes. Everyone has to be back at midnight tomorrow so it looks as though we may get away on the 12th. I hope there won't be anymore delays.

August 17, 1945.

As you can see I'm still waiting at my "report" address and the way things look I'll be here till the end of the month. I'm hoping to stay sane. This bloody army sure gets things mixed up. This is the most hopeless situation I have ever gotten into. They don't seem to know the score or at very least, are unable to give the reason for the many delays.

Last night I got back from a very worthwhile five days in Scotland. I spent Sunday in Edinburgh and attended service at St. Giles Cathedral. I had to queue up to get in. I was never more disappointed in a service. Just one service like that in Canada and I wouldn't have a congregation for the next Sunday. In the afternoon, I paid a visit to the Firth of Forth Bridge. It was quite a sight and thrill. In the evening I took a quick tour of the city.

Monday found me in Aberdeen. It quite impressed me. I think it's the nicest city I have seen over here. All the houses are made of granite, and when the sun shines they just sparkle. On Tuesday I went to Inverness. The train passed through some wonderful highland country. I just spent four hours here, then took a bus to Fort William. This trip took me through the lake country. I had a most interesting chat with a Scot on the bus, who gave me a grand bunch of white heather to take home. Fort William wasn't much to see, still since it is the centre of the Highlands, I didn't want to miss it. I spent the night there in a very sporty officers' club.

About 5:00 a.m. we were awakened to the news of the end of the war in the Pacific. The place went wild. We arrived in Glasgow the day after V-J Day. It was very crowded and everybody was hitting the high spots celebrating. Along with another officer, I went down to the centre of the city. It was quite a sight. Young and old were dancing in the streets. Every corner had its piper and here and there one could see a long-saved bottle of whiskey dying a quick death in the company of a dozen Scots. Somehow I just felt like a spectator. My day of victory will be celebrated when I know I'm home.

I took the train Thursday morning and got back to camp at 9:00 p.m. the same day. I enjoyed seeing Scotland. It really had some wonderful scenery. This continual hanging around is getting us down. While no definite date had been given, we are told we will get away by the end of the month. Having suffered from four cancellations, the pill of disappointment gets harder to swallow.

This was the last letter from Europe. The Padre finally left England at the end of August 1945 and returned to a happy and joyful reunion with his family.

We Shall Remember Him

Someone once said that a man has achieved success who has lived well, laughed often and loved much; who has gained the respect of intelligent men and the love of little children; who has filled his niche and accomplished his task; who has left the world better than he found it, whether by an improved poppy, a perfect poem, or a rescued soul; who has never lacked appreciation of earth's beauty or failed to express it; who has always looked for the best in others and given the best he had; whose life was an inspiration; whose memory a benediction ...

A Man of Action

The Royal Guard at Sandringham Was All Dave's

We were up in Norfolk in Northern England. 'Baker' company was holed up in a castle called Hillington Hall. While we were there, we were invited out a number of times to dinner at the homes of several lords and ladies. At one of these teas there was a lady-in-waiting to the Queen. She was Irish. The Padre, who was Irish himself, struck up a conversation with her. During the course of their talk, the thought came up that it would be a grand idea if the Irish Regiment guarded the King and Queen, who were coming to Sandringham for a holiday. Dave thought it was a fantastic idea. The idea went to warhouse. The reply was that, it was the craziest idea anyone had thought of. Who in their right mind would put wild Canadians in charge of such a duty! Dave wouldn't take that for an answer. He went right back and persisted. Finally, he won out and it was the first time in history that any Canadian Regiment had ever guarded the King and Queen. If it hadn't been for Dave, it would never have happened. The Colonel was dumbfounded when word came back to select one major, three captains and a hundred men to be taken off everything so that they could be trained for this guard duty.

He Was Totally Convinced That the Padre Preached the Whole Service Directly at Him

I remember one of Dave's church services when he really tore a strip off the entire Regiment. The service was held after a particularly rowdy night. The evening before, some guy coming out of the wet canteen had bumped into the Padre and not recognizing him, muttered some choice words in Dave's direction. From that elevated pulpit looking down at everyone, he suddenly tore up his sermon and said, "In reverence, I start the service by repeating what was said to me last night." Wham! The Padre started in and the words he used you'll never find in the Bible! He was so mad that the veins in his neck stood out like guitar strings. He had the men in that Regiment talking to themselves for weeks after. The officers always sat in the front rows with the men. I walked out with one of the officers, who was one of the ones who was particularly boozed up the night before. He was totally convinced that the Padre preached the whole sermon directly at him. He was sure that the Padre didn't look at anyone else in the entire church! Did he floor them that day!

A Man of Dedication

They Were His Pals

Of all our dead only two, at the most, were never found by the Padre and his staunch assistants. All the others were searched out on the battlefields after we had passed by, (and at times before we had passed on), and their bodies were given an honourable burial by a man to whom they had mean't far more than just another soldier. They were his pals and it showed in his voice as he read the service over them.

We can never forget meeting the Padre in Tomba di Pesaro, just after the breakthrough of the Gothic Line. He had spent endless hours under a hot sun, searching out our fallen lads and preparing them for burial. Veterans of that campaign need no words to describe what the completion of such a task implies. But there was the Padre before us, sweating and near physical and mental exhaustion, still with that Irish smile for us and the proud word that not one of our men was then unaccounted for. After a couple of words on their magnificent work that day, he turned away and carried on with the preparation of a cemetery and an appropriate service. None of us needed to see the citation to know why he was awarded the Cross ... in each of our minds there is a different and perfectly adequate reason.

The Padre Recited the Hebrew Prayers Over the Boys

It was the 20th of December — it must have been 'C' company. They ran into some difficulty. The Padre poked his nose into the place where we had been staying and told us that a number of lads from 'C' company had been clipped. He said that there were about eight men, including a couple of our Jewish lads. Apparently one of the Jewish lads had just arrived that day. The two lads stuck together. When we got there in the morning all eight of them were lying in an area no bigger than a living room. When we picked them up, they were so heavy that we had to put them on boards and float them down a little bit of a canal. They were buried right there and then. For the two Jewish lads the Padre recited the Hebrew prayers in Hebrew. To me this was remarkable. I wrote to the mother of one of the lads and told her how he was buried with all the proper prayers and rites.

He Would Travel Miles to the Field Hospitals to Visit the Boys

The Padre would travel miles to the field hospitals to visit the boys. Literally thousands of miles to any hospital where there was thought to be an Irish lad; from Bari to Salerno and from Ravenna to Jesi, Rome or Naples. There was never a hospital that Davey missed in his endless travels, bearing mail, cigarettes and comforts for the lads who had been hit, or who were ill. He would go back miles to visit men so badly wounded that they couldn't write. He worked night after night, just writing letters. Imagine composing letters to families of men who were not going to make it. I never heard of anyone who received a letter under these circumstances that wasn't in full praise of Dave's concern and thoughtfulness. He carried out that job in a most faithful and dedicated fashion. He would tuck himself away for hours, and even days and carry out this task. This was only part of his job.

In Many Ways Dave Was the Irish Regiment

In many ways Dave was the Irish Regiment to an awful lot of the men. When there were problems, he would say *Bring them to me, I'll look after you.* Looking at it in retrospect, it is so hard to understand how he found the time to take on all of these responsibilities. It didn't matter what it was – the man was important. It didn't matter to the Padre who you were – Protestant, Catholic, Jew, Christian or Atheist – he always had time to talk to you and help with your problems. He would drop everything else to administer to a man's needs. He turned nobody down and said nothing about what he did. There wasn't another Padre like him. I don't believe that he ever had an easy day.

A Man With a Sense of Humour

That Will Be 50 Lire

You know he would lay down the law to us in the R.A.P. Everytime you would swear – that was 50 lire in his "swear box." One day they brought in a Cape Breton Islander who got clipped. The Padre was wearing that leather jerkin and you couldn't see his pips to tell he was a Captain, or for that matter, a Padre. You know, he had on a steel helmet, dirty boots etc. Every other word from this Cape Breton lad was a study in profanity. The Padre asked him what had happened. He says "One of those f ...... bakalite gernades." "Oh," said the Padre, "Is that a new type?"

The lad says, "What the f ...... is wrong with you f ...... Irishmen anyway?"

"Old Bucko is standing off in the corner saying, "700 lire, 750 lire, 800 lire ......"

The lad starts to look around. "What the f ...... is he talking about? 700 lire, 750 lire?" Finally the lad was tipped off that this was the Padre of the Irish Regiment. "Oh," he says, "I'm sorry, sir."

The Padre says, "I hope you have your wallet with you young fellow."
The Place erupted.

Wake Up the Man On Your Left

I recall the Padre conducting a special service while we were in Heerenveen, Holland, near the end of our active service. The church was filled to capacity, with the Regiment in full attendance along with the entire population of Heerenveen. A young soldier beside me fell asleep during the service. The Padre happened to glance up from the pulpit, noticed the lad dozing off, stopped the service and bellowed out "C.D. wake up the man on your left. Belt him a good one."

A Man of Courage

Where the Stuff Was Flying That's Where Dave Was

I remember walking with him one night. It was winter time and the boys were strung out across the top of this gully. I said to him, "Why are you not afraid?" He said, "I'm afraid." Nothing more. You know, I saw my share of comrades killed. We were all pretty damn close. We were like family. The Padre saw them all. He was always in the R.A.P. with the M.O. I saw him covered in gore. That's where he wanted to be because that's where he was needed. He was needed by the men and officers alike. Where the stuff was flying that's where Dave was.

He Threw Himself On Top of the Lad

He was always at the R.A.P. intercepting the wounded and dying. He did a wonderful job. I remember a lad who had a serious "sucking" wound. He was in bad shape. They were patching him up in a thick barn and Jerry was shelling us pretty heavily. At one point a shell landed on the roof. Everything was falling in. The Padre threw himself on top of that lad to protect him with no thought for himself. There were two different types of decorations: an immediate and periodical. Dave got a periodical. He could have got an immediate everytime we went into action. He took some great risks but it was clear that they had to be taken. There was no fuss ... he just went ahead and did what had to be done.

There Was the Padre Yelling 'Kamarade'

Not only did the Padre go up to the line, but I recall a time when he went beyond the line. Somebody had really 'snafu'd.' The Padre, M.O., Steve and a couple of others went up with the wrong coordinates and ended up half a mile beyond the Jerry lines. When we got up there we looked around for a well built house for the R.A.P. The Padre picked one out and we all pitched in to clean out the manure and dirt. We sat down to wait for the M.O. to arrive. An hour or two went by and nobody showed up. By that time it was dark. We had both carriers with us. Evening came and everything was quiet. The Padre went outside, but soon returned. He told us not to panic, but he could hear Germans just outside. He told us to roll up our sleeping bags and kits and load up the carriers. He told us to start them both at the same time and go. We didn't know where the hell we were going. The Padre was sitting up front yelling 'Kamarade! Kamarade!' We got back all right but he told me afterwards that he was afraid that some of our own boys might pick us up quicker than Jerry.

The Padre Never Flinched

How could he ever do the things that he did? Everybody was tired and here was a man doing double duty. I was on one burial party with the Padre. We had German prisoners digging the graves. All of a sudden Jerry started shelling us and the Germans jumped into the holes, leaving us up on top. We soon got them out and everybody was saying, 'Hold off! Hold off!' The Padre stood there and gave his service no matter how many were coming in. Just after that we were advancing on Cassino. A tank had been knocked out and the crew were crawling up towards a bank for cover. The whole area was mined. The guys rushed headlong into a cave in the side of a hill, because Jerry was starting to shell again. Again I remember that Padre, because he was the last one in. He was standing right in the opening of the cave making sure that all the men were inside. Not a shell came near that opening. That was the thing. The Padre never flinched under these kinds of circumstances. You know he deserved more than the Military Cross, I'll tell you.

A Man Most Loved and Admired

I Never Met a Man Like Him Nor Have I Since

He was a most remarkable guy, a wonderful guy, that we all took to right from the start. His philosophy was great and he left a tremendous impression on me. I never met a man like him, nor have I since. I tried to pattern my life after him. I was very close to him all the way. I don't think that it was the things that everyone knew he did, but the things that he did that nobody knew about. Everyone knew how great he was. When we used to come out of the line, it was rest for us but not for him. He used to go to his tent and write next-of-kin letters. Many nights I went to his tent and just watched while he completed those very difficult letters. They weren't *'form'* letters. He wrote each honestly and sincerely, because he knew the men so well and their wives and mothers. I'm sure many of those letters have been kept to this day.

No Guy Is That Great But He Was

People will say that any man who says that he is never afraid is a liar. The Padre was too busy to be afraid. To my knowledge he buried every man in our Unit who was killed. I saw him organize burial parties, and go out and put our casualties into gas capes ... many times there was not much left of a man. It was very sad. Many of your friends were with you one day and gone the next. It must have been very difficult for him because they were all his friends. That was a thing with him that he wanted to do. It was almost unbelievable. People may listen to you and say that it's a lot of balls – no guy is that great, but he was. He was great in everything that he did. He was great on the sportsfield and battlefield. They will never replace him. The Padre was a Prince.

He Was a Man to Be Admired

There was a young Catholic lad who had been hit and was dying. He asked the Padre to take his confession. He comforted him right there until he passed away. They all wanted the Padre to be with them in their last hours ... it didn't matter what faith or creed. I recall that we had brought another lad into the R.A.P. who had stepped on a mine, He was badly dismembered. He was going quickly. The M.O. gave him a needle and rallied him for a few minutes. He was preparing to give him another one. The Padre tapped him on the shoulder as much as to say, "Leave him to me now." He held the lad in his arms and comforted him until he passed away. I have met many men both in and out of the cloth and I have never met another man like him. He was a man to be admired.

A Man of God

Without Question He Was One of the Best Padres the Canadian Army Ever Produced

Dave and I served together as padres in the Fifth Division. I got to know him very well at that time. I found him a loyal friend and confidant. Without question he was one of the best padres the Canadian Army ever produced. He knew and loved the men whom he served. I know this from personal experience and observation, during battle where he demonstrated his dedication and concern for all ranks under his spiritual care. The Lord's work, in the Canadian Forces was always very dear to him. His contribution was of the highest order.

A Man Who Served God by Serving His Children

Dave Rowland was a man who served God by serving his children. He was a man of integrity with a heart full of compassion for all those in need who were drawn to his attention. He translated religion into deeds; he transmitted to all who came in contact with him a determination that the Church must ever be searching for ways to assist the unfortunate. Although he was a teacher, preacher and exemplar to the children and adults of York Memorial Presbyterian Church, he still found time to be associated with many community projects. We will never know how many heavy burdens he lightened, how many tired spirits he refreshed, nor how many broken hearts he healed by the material assistance and spiritual medicine that he so generously dispensed. No matter was too trivial for him and no case too onerous. In war and in peace he served.

The Irish Regiment of Canada: A Brief History

The Irish Regiment of Canada was one of the younger regiments of a young nation. The Regiment was in existence less than fifty years after the creation of the Dominion of Canada, and served with distinction in both world wars. Its destiny is already firmly interwoven with that of the Canadian people.

Gazetted on October 15, 1915, the 110th (Irish) Regiment of Canada came into existence through the endeavours of the Irish Club and the Irish Rifle Club, two Toronto organizations formed to offer an opportunity for fellowship among the local citizens of Irish descent. A battalion of the new Regiment proceeded overseas in 1916, and there, unfortunately was broken up to reinforce other regiments already in the field; however, a record was kept of the personnel of this, the 208th Battalion and of the 108th Sportsmen's Battalion which followed it overseas from the same source. The Regimental Colours were deposited in Belfast Cathedral during the war, and remained there until a party was despatched to bring them home to Toronto at the close of hostilities. About 60% of the personnel of the Regiment were killed or wounded during this period, and the list of battle honours inscribed on the colours will serve to indicate the actions in which they fought: Arras 1917-1918, Hill 70, Ypres 1917, Amiens, Hindenburg Line, Pursuit to Mons, Scarpe 1918, Drocourt-Queant, Canal du Nord, France and Flanders' 18.

During the ensuing years of peacetime activities the Regiment was maintained as a Machine-Gun Battalion of Canada's Non-Permanent Active Militia. A succession of enthusiastic and influential Commanding Officers succeeded in bringing the Regiment into a position of distinction in Toronto through the development of a distinguished dress, a pipe band, and careful training, all of which succeeded in forcing the Highland units of the city to make way for a unit of equal prominence and ability. The kilt of saffron was adopted in 1931 and this, together with the caubeen and the hat-badge consisting of a silver harp mounted on the five-pointed Star of Independence in gold, surmounted by the Imperial Crown, with the motto beneath, 'Fior Go Bas' was the distinguishing mark of the Regiment since that date.

In August 1939, the Irish Regiment of Canada was called upon to provide detachments for the guarding of a number of R.C.A.F. depots and airfields. At this time 200 of all ranks were mobilized. However, it was not until June 1940, that the regiment received general mobilization orders for active service. After completing basic training, the Regiment was ordered to the east coast of Canada, where they spent over a year in a coastal defence role.

In October 1942, the 1st Battalion proceeded overseas, and came to rest in that inevitable destination of all Canadian troops, Aldershot. Shortly after the arrival of the Regiment in England, the organization of an Armoured Division was changed and the Regiment was transferred from the Fourth to the Fifth Division, where they became part of the 11th Brigade. In the final stages of training at King's Lynn, in Norfolk, the King graciously consented to have a Canadian guard at Sandringham and this single honour was bestowed on the Regiment.

In November 1943, the Regiment proceeded with the remainder of the Division to Italy.

After a period in the static fronts near Orsogna and Arielli in the late winter of 1943-44 as well as a time spent in a bold role at Mount Cifalco, just north of Cassino, during April and May of 1944, the Regiment moved with the rest of the First Canadian Corps into the Hitler Line. Here with the armour of the British Columbia Dragoons it exploited, until the 1st of June, the breach made in the line on the night of May 23 by the West Nova Scotia Regiment. This point lay midway between Pontecorvo and Aquino and the exploitation carried the Irish across the Melfa River to the important town of Ceprano, at which the Liri River is crossed by Highway 6. Since the highway had been cut at this point, the attack was carried forward to a point not far from Frosinone, where a final consolidation was made on the first day of June.

At the close of the summer the Regiment participated in the breakthrough of the Gothic Line. With a squadron of the 8th New Brunswick Hussars a breach was made in the line at Montecchio, a little inland from the Adriatic coastal town of Pesaro. Hill 120 and 111 of the Gothic Line at this point were captured on September 1 and from there the Regiment moved on to a series of actions, among which might be mentioned Tomba di Pesaro and a particularly difficult assault on the town of Coriano near Cattolica, the capture of which brought messages of congratulations from the Army Commander and Winston Churchill. The obstinate citadel fell to the Irish after a forty-eight hour battle this after repeated attacks by other units in the area had been unsuccessful. Its fall enabled the Eighth Army to move out onto the plains of Northern Italy. The crossing of the Savio, Munio and Lamone Rivers brought the Regiment in December, to the Senio River north of Ravenna, from whence they were recalled, after some extensive fighting, to prepare for departure to northwestern Europe. The Irish left Italy in January of 1945 and in March moved into the line south of Arnhem. After the fall of that city to the 49th British Division, the Irish were part of the pursuit to drive to the Zuider Zee. En route, at the little village of Otterloo, just north of Arnhem, a heavy German counter-attack was concentrated on the Unit, which was at the time in a reserve position. A stout battle ensued and with the aid of daring sallies on the part of the flame-throwing platoon, the attack was repulsed. The pressure on Divisional headquarters which itself was visited by German troops, was removed completely. The final action in which the Regiment participated was the drive to Delfzijl, on the Ems River in northern Holland. After some days the German garrison there surrendered to the Regiment. 1300 German soldiers were removed from the town on May 2 ... rather a formidable opposition for a single regiment already depleted somewhat in strength through previous engagements.

In December 1945, the Irish Regiment left Holland, where they had spent the postwar months, and after a short stay in England returned to Canada. Toronto welcomed home the 1st Battalion in January 1946.

During the Regiment's absence the 2nd Battalion (Reserve) had maintained a training programme, first for those underage for active service and then as part of the home defence scheme which trained men unfit for active service. The Regiment became once more a single unit, training a nucleus of officers and N.C.O.'s at weekly training periods. Affiliated with it were the Cadet Corps of Northern Vocational and Malvern Collegiate in Toronto. These units paraded to the Fort York Armoury, the headquarters of the Irish Regiment, for their annual inspection, and from their ranks the future personnel of the Regiment were drawn. A flourishing Veterans' Association kept close contact with the Regiment and periodically brought together large numbers of men who served with the Unit at various times. 1951 found the Regiment an accredited and firmly established part of Canada's militia and the honour of being affiliated with the Royal Ulster Rifles was one in which the Regiment took great pride.

In the 1960's the Irish Regiment of Canada fell victim to the Liberal government's decision to submerge Canada's militia in the National Defense Reorganization. The Regimental colours were deposited in the Padre's church where they remain today.

Padre Dave Rowland with King George VI at Sandringham Castle.

Officers who formed the Royal Guard at Sandringham Castle with the Royal Family.

Princesses Elizabeth and Margaret inspect the Irish.

*he Queen inspects the Royal Guard
at Sandringham.*

*Officers of the Royal Guard posed for this
informal photo following the church service
at Sandringham.*

The Queen and Princesses Elizabeth and Margaret officially inspect the Irish Guard.

*In Holland after "V.E. Day". From left
Brig. Ian Johnston, General Crerar,
Captain G. Hargan, Lt.Col. L.H.C. Payne.*

Toronto 1940

*A hand picked group comprised of one major, three captains, Padre Rowland, and one hu[n]
dred men drilled intensively for a full month prior to guarding the King and Queen while t[hey]
were on holiday.*

STAR WEEKLY

TORONTO ★
SEPTEMBER 27, 1941

10 CENTS

Toronto Mayor Bob Saunders greeting Col. George MacCartney and other members of
the Irish on their arrival in New York City, January 15, 1946.

Toronto reunion-1944, from left — Rosemary LaPrairie, Pte. Swire, Irene Lowrey, Pt
Wise and Mary Gordon.

Inseparable companions. Baker Company prior to the break through of the Hitler line, Italy, May, 1944.

Holland 1945

Colonel Bill Elder and wife, Lea, along with their host, Mr. A. Halma, during a spring visit to Holland. 1982.

A crowd of twenty thousand families turned out at the CNE Colliseum to welcome home the Irish, January 16, 1946.

The Chaplaincy Service in Review

In 1948, H/Major Walter T. Steven M.A., B.Th., with the assistance of a committee of Toronto Chaplains, produced a narrative entitled 'In This Sign', to acknowledge the role played by Canada's chaplains in both Canadian Theaters of War. In that dissertation is found a synopsis of the history of the chaplaincy service:

"The evidence is clear that chaplains held the King's commission in the British Army since 1662. The actual ministry of religion in the armed forces of Britain and other lands is, of course, far more ancient. In medieval times when kings and knights rode out to battle, the priest, half-soldier and half-saint, rode with them to the fray.

It is a far cry from Friar Tuck to the highly organized Chaplain Service of a modern army, but the ministry of both finds its roots in some deep, often ill-defined hunger in the human heart.

In the England of those days, neither Roman Catholics nor Noncomformists had a place in official religious arrangements, and it was nearly two centuries after the first commissioning of chaplains before other than clergy of the established Church of England received appointments. Provision for the spiritual welfare of the troops was not neglected, however, for we learn that 'the articles of war of that date ordered all chaplains to say prayers daily for the troops. Absence from these prayers was published by loss of a day's pay.'

It appears, however, that the custom of daily prayers ceased after a few years. The Christian cause was at a low ebb in all denominations in the late seventeenth and eighteenth centuries. The materialistic traffic in chaplaincies, for convenience or profit, became so prevalent that by the end of the eighteenth century, a special Warrant was issued which stated, 'no sales, exchange or transfer of commissions by the present chaplains should be permitted after the 25th of December 1796, unless the application for that purpose should have been previously made; and in this interval that no chaplaincy should be sold for more than was given for it, not should the purchaser have any claim to sell the same again.' It is probable that this drastic revision of a corrupt sytem was closely related to the moral, spiritual and social awakening under John Wesley and his friends that was shaking the Britain of those days, and out of which many reforms grew.

It was in 1796 also that the regimental system for appointing chaplains was abolished and a chaplain-general commenced to superintend the Department. It is interesting to note that only with the outbreak of World War II did the Canadian Chaplain Service shake itself from this regimental system.

By dint of much controversy and on the old principle of trial and error, the Chaplain Service progressed until the year 1829 when the decline set in. The office of Chaplain-General was abolished and by the year 1843 there were only five staff chaplains in commission. By 1844 an all-time low had been reached and a reorganization commenced. Strangely enough, the title then adopted for the Chief was the one which has become so familiar in the Canadian Army, Principal Chaplain. Two years later, the office of Chaplain-General was revived and put on a satisfactory basis in the matter of pay.

The Crimean War had a marked influenced on the Chaplains' Department. During the war the staff of clergy was greatly increased and in November 1858, the present Royal Army Chaplains' Department was formed. Two marked changes were introduced at this time. The chaplains were divided for rating into four classes under the Chaplain-General who held the rank of Major-General. Chaplains of the first class were in the rank of colonel; the second class, lieutenant-colonel; the third class, major; the fourth class, captain.

The most important change, however, was that clergy not members of the Church of England came into the service. Nineteen Roman Catholic priests and five Presbyterian ministers were brought into the establishment of the Army as commissioned chaplains. It should be added that members of these denominations had been paid as acting-chaplains since the year 1836, but in 1858 they received commissions as fully recognized chaplains.

At least one Roman Catholic priest was an Army Chaplain much earlier than 1836. Alexander Macdonell was a Highland priest, deeply concerned with the sufferings of the Gaelic speaking men from Glengarry who had been evicted from their holdings by the oppressive land tenure system of their day. Macdonell was largely instrumental in organizing his Highlanders into a regiment to fight for the King in Ireland. Later his influence secured them land grants and passage to Canada. In the war of 1812, he was mainly responsible for organizing a new Glengarry Regiment which saw action in fourteen general engagements.

He was a man of great frame. He stood six feet four inches, and used to say that every man of his name should be either a priest or a soldier. Many stories are told of his sturdy manhood and his unique loyalty to the crown. The tale that he went into battle with a sword in one hand and a Bible in the other, though most descriptive, is probably apocryphal. The story probably has a common origin with the one which Sir John A. Macdonald was fond of telling. His story is that as the troops advanced across the ice from Prescott toward Ogdensburg on February 22, 1813, in full view of the enemy a Presbyterian minister, Bible in hand, marched on one flank with Chaplain Macdonell on the other flank holding aloft the Cross. One man showed signs of weakness and a desire to turn back. When warnings failed to bolster his courage, the priest excommunicated him on the spot! It was a saying amongst the Highlanders that "where Maigshster Alastair (his Gaelic name) led there never foot went back." The other typical story, however, seems authentic. When Ogdensburg was taken, a wounded soldier named Ross was carried into an inn kept by Yankee sympathizers. On their refusal to produce brandy for his Presbyterian friend, Macdonell used his great strength to kick down the tap-room door, and that day more than the sick men had brandy.

Father Macdonell became the first Roman Catholic Bishop of Upper Canada. He was a noted soldier, missionary and prelate a great loyalist, and a tolerant Christian who numbered many Protestants amongst his friends. He also became a member of the Legislative Council of the Province. He died at the age of eighty in 1840.

The Canadian Chaplain Service inherits much of its position in the Army from the struggles of the parent service. The nineteenth century saw great strides in Britain in the matter of religious liberty. This is seen within the Chaplain Service and within the established Church. Army chaplains working in camps and garrison churches came in conflict, for instance, with the parochial clergy, and at the time of General Peel's Revised Warrant of 1858, the question of the legal status of Army chaplains had to be considered. An eminent legal authority decided that '*a Chaplain to the Forces commissioned by the Queen can excerise in England, towards Her Majesty's troops exclusively those spiritual functions for which he is appointed, without the license of the Bishop or the assent of the incumbent.*' Jurisdiction was not settled at that time, however, nor indeed until the Army Chaplains' Act of 1868 was passed. This act enables the Crown '*to set out by metes and bounds a precinct, and to declare the station, for all the ecclesiastical purposes of the Act, to be an extra-parochial district.*' ''[1]

In practical terms, the role of the chaplain was a multi-faceted one. Simply stated, he was responsible for looking after the regiment and its needs. He was there to listen and give advice. Individual problems, domestic problems, soldier problems, would involve a tremendous amount of his time. In military terms, officers issued the orders; men in the ranks followed them. The lines of responsibility were abundantly clear. The chaplain's responsibilities were more universal as the spiritual, social and physical well-being of *all* men fell under his jurisdiction.

Canadian Chaplains Remember

Canadian Chaplains of many faiths served in the various Second World War Theatres with distinction. The publisher regrets that only a small number of Padres are included on these few pages. It would be a privilege to recognize the individual contributions made by hundreds of war-time Chaplains. Though modest in its size this section is intended to serve as a tribute to Army, Navy, and Airforce Padres of different denominations.

Remembrance / Major Stewart East

The Peace Movement in 1982

Since the War in Europe and Asia ended in 1945 there have been wars but no world CONFLICT. For this we give thanks to God, praying that the real fear of a Neuclear Holocast will CONTINUE to hold back the dogs of war.

Of course all Christians favour universal disarmament and the establishing of undefended borders, such as Canadians enjoy with their good neighbour to the south. Unhappily all the world is not yet a neighbourhood and other Hitlers will arise and other peoples will come under their spell. They are the enemies of PEACE. May God save us from any peace movement which encourages them and makes necessary another unnecessary war.

"Worse than injustice", someone wrote is *"Justice without a sword in her hand."*

Remembrance Day 1982

For me, Remembrance Day is an occasion for REPENTANCE: a day of remembering that Jesus was *the Prince of Peace* — that in the divine plan wars are unnecessary, only becoming necessary when among men and women of goodwill there is apathy, ignorance and insufferable disobedience. The war of 1939-45 was of all wars the *"NECESSARY* unnecessary War."* — For this we must repent for the same sins are with us still.

I have great respect for the true Christian pacifist but I have little respect for the cynics who infiltrate the body politic in the name of peace, making it difficult for democracies to exercise the kind of police action which can stop a war before it begins.

While serving as Minister of Wesley United Church in Jarvis, Ont. Rev. S.B. East entered the army as a lieutenant in the 41st Field Brigade, (Battery Regiment) and joined the chaplaincy service in July 1940.

In 1944 Mr. East was appointed as an assistant senior chaplain and in 1945 he became senior chaplain.

On October 6, 1944, as chaplain with the 48th Highlanders in Italy, Honorary Captain Stewart B. East was promoted to the rank of Honorary Major.

From Italy came the following story:

"Captain East, with his leg cut by shrapnel from a bursting shell, disregarded his own danger and cared for the wounded and dying until ordered to retire."

Throughout the Sicilian and Italian campaigns, Rev. Stewart East was always on the scene where he felt his presence was most needed, caring for his charges where the fighting was the fiercest. and acting as stretcher bearer when necessary.

In the papers of that day we find headings:

"Padre East dug grave unaided to spare weary men from task."

"One grand man" is Padre with 48th in Sicily."

"Padre in Sicily earns high praise" (United Church Observer, Sept. 1/43)

"48th fire eating Padre ignores wound to aid men."

Rev. East was twice decorated. In September 1944, he was awarded the Military Cross. For more than 4 years, stories of his fearless devotion to duty under fire excited and thrilled countless Canadians in Italy. He was their friend in act as well as in word. He exemplified his faith in God and his example was in great inspiration to the men.

Lt. Col. John Weir Foote

Lt. Col. John Weir Foote was Canada's 14th Victoria Cross winner of the Second World War, and he was the first Canadian chaplain ever to receive the Victoria Cross.

The gallantry of the former chaplian of the Royal Hamilton Light Infantry (Wentworth Regiment) was shown in no sudden blaze of violent action, but coolly and calmly through eight hours of the gruelling, terrible battle of Dieppe, in which, says the official citation, "with utter disregard for his own safety he exposed himself to an inferno of fire and saved many lives by his gallant efforts."

Then at the end of his trial by fire, he climbed from the landing craft that was to have taken him to safety, and walked courageously into the German positions, that he might be taken prisoner and so minister to his men whose fate for the next three years was to be barbed wire and chains.

With other prisoners Padre Foote was marched to a temporary camp. Before long he found himself placed in Offlag 7B, a camp reserved for officers. Here were provided capture parcels and food parcels from the International Red Cross.

In the camp, Lt. Col. Foote had the fellowship of two British chaplains captured at Dunkirk, one Church of England and one Roman Catholic. The co-operation he received from them, Lt. Col. Foote wrote home, was the best that could be imagined and made the work much more satisfactory than it would otherwise have been. The little prison chapel was constantly in use, personal interviews and services following each other throughout the day. Being a padre, Lt. Col. Foote was one of few allowed to visit the men in shackles.

Padre Foote was released from Offlage 7B on April 25, 1945, by the British Grenadier Guards.

Remembrance / Ven. E.S. Light

It was early evening in late March of 1945, I was on my way to the de-briefing room at our air base at Holthorpe, Yorkshire, the home station for 420 and 425 Squadrons of Number 6 Group RCAF. The squadrons were returning from a mission over enemy territory. Suddenly I noticed a Lancaster bomber trailing and flying at tree top height. It crashed in flames and disintegrated in a nearby field. I rushed over to see if there were any survivors and an airman called to me, "Padre" he said, "I think this fellow is still alive." In the fading light I knelt beside him and held his hand. His pulse was very weak. I told him I was the Padre and that medical help was on the way. He was conscious but it was obvious he was seriously injured and he seemed to sense that he was dying. He gasped out a plea for some kind of reassurance. *"Padre"* he said, *"is there a heaven? Is God for real?"* "How" I said to myself, "could I articulate the faith of the resurrection and of God's assurance of eternity to a young man who's life was slipping fast?" In my tunic pocket I carried a small crucifix that had been given to me by my friend Father Tom O'Brien when I was posted overseas in June of 1944. I took it out and placed it in his hand, and as he felt the figure of Christ on the cross, I told him that God's only son had suffered and died, but the otherside of the crucifix was the empty cross, a symbol of God's victory over death and the promise of eternal life. He held the crucifix tightly in his hand and as the darkness descended his young life came to an end. When he was buried along with his crew a few days later, the crucifix was buried with him.

Thirty seven years have passed since that evening in a Yorkshire field, but I remember it often and it recalls for me the names and faces of so many other young men who "shall not grow old as we who are left grow old."

On the 11th of November I think of that young airman who's name I never knew, as he was from a squadron of a nearby base. I believe it is never inappropriate to remember with gratitude and sorrow that young man and countless thousands like him, but if the act of remembrance is to be something more than just a traditional and prefunctory two minutes observance before a granite, then individuals and nations and governments must give top priority to the elimination of war as a means of acheiving political, financial or geographical objectives.

Enlisted in the RCAF in October 1941 in air crew — too young to be a padre at that time. He was transferred to the chaplaincy service of the RCAF in late 1942, served briefly as chaplain at Toronto and Calgary, and early in 1943 posted to #2 Bombing and Gunnery School at Mossbank, Saskatchewan as padre. In the spring of 1944, Padre Light joined the SFTS training school at Claresholm, Alberta.

He was posted overseas in June 1944 and served as padre at the Canadian Bomber Base at Holthorpe in Yorkshire with 425 Squadron (Allouttes) and 420 Squadron

(Snow Owls). In the late spring of 1945, Padre Light was posted to a Spitfire Fighter Wing (RCAF) in Germany, and served with the occupation force until October 1945 on posting back to Canada.

His very extensive post-war experience includes service as Command Chaplain with the Canadian Air Division (RCAF) in Europe, based at Metz, France; Director of Chaplain Services (Protestant) RCASF, Air Foce Headquarters, Ottawa; and Chaplain General (Protestant) for the Canadian Armed Forces, National Defence Headquarters, Ottawa.

Ven. E.S. Light retired from military service in 1968 and was appointed General Secretary of the Anglican Church of Canada (1968-1979). In 1980 he was appointed Executive Secretary of the Provincial Synod of Ontario.

Remembrance / Padre-David Monson

My friend Dave Rowland helped to find Jews hidden away by Dutch christian families. Once informed, I would make arrangements with the Jewish agency that the individuals rescued be properly looked after.

I remember well how Major Rowland met with me the day before Passover, 1945, in order that Jewish members of his regiment could be present at the sizeable Seder in Nymegen.

The two of us discussed the need to seek official permission for Jewish survivors: tradesmen and artisans, to emmigrate to Canada. As usual, Dave did his part.

Rabbi Capt. D.A. Monson served overseas as Chaplain of the Jewish personnel of the Canadian Armed Forces in the European Theatre.

H/Capt. Monson functioned as Jewish Padre with the 3RD Canadian Division Headquarters. He arrived in England in March, 1944. By late summer of the same year, Padre Monson was posted to Holland.

Remembrance / Robert L. Seaborn

The Most Reverend Robert L. Seaborn, Bishop Ordinary (Anglican) to the Canadian Forces. Enlisted on August 8, 1942 and served as Padre of the 3rd Bn. Queen's Own Rifles at Niagara-on-the-Lake and from October to April 1943 at Debert, N.S.

Posted to Aldershot, England in the spring of 1943, he became Padre to the 1st Bn. The Canadian Scottish Regiment, (7th Brigade, 3rd Division) At 0800 hours on "D" Day, June 6th, 1944, in France. Padre Seaborn served in France, Belgium, Holland and finally Germany until the end of the hostilities.

He was awarded the French Croix de Guerre (avec Etoile de Vermeil) re Normandy.

H / Major R.F. Sneyd, C.D.

It was not until April 1945 that I became closely associated with Padre Rowland. On my first day as senior chaplain of 5 Armoured Division in Holland I paid a visit to the Irish and Dave. I had learned from "Chips" Drury that we were going into action the next day. Major Dean Johnston who had been the senior chaplain of the division all the way through Italy, made my task very easy because he had been such an excellent organizer.

The second battle of Arnhem was fought the next day. Our division went over the pontoon bridges on the east of the city and drove on westward to the town of Oterloo. It was exhilarating to be with these men who had come up from Italy and helped to free this city in which there was such a disaster a few months before. The Irish had two men killed by snipers near Oterloo and Padre Rowland told me that the local domini wanted him to bury these men in the cemetery of his kirk, near some British paratroopers. I gave permission for this knowing that the location, was somewhat irregular.

I left our forward troops and returned to Arnhem for a burial service for some of our men who died at our field dressing station. On my way back I met Capt. Don Wagner from my own church in Toronto who told me that he had just received the message that 3000 Germans were retreating from Appledoorn and were heading for Amsterdam. This meant passing through Oterloo. Very shortly after, I met 5 Div. HQ. speeding forward to take up a position near the village.

That was hectic night, for back in Arnhem we were cut off in our contact with the troops ahead. A battle was raging. First thing next morning I met many prisoners and casualties as I returned to the location of the day before. The whole scene was typical of all the confusion, destruction and horror of war. Padre Rowland was in the domini's home by the church when the German troop penetrated the Canadian positions. He told me that he had actually seen enemy soldiers outside their windows. The two of us were very busy with the grim task, which fall to a padre's lot after battle, and we buried our casualties next to the graves which we had used the day before. Very seldom are you able to do a numerical count after battle, but we found the German losses were exactly four times heavier than ours. The head of the Dutch Red Cross asked me for any duties they could perform and I gave him the very onerous task of burying all the German dead. This freed us of a lot of work and documentation.

Very shortly after the above action the whole division was pulled out and given the objective of clearing the northeast section of Holland heading toward the seacoast town of Delfzile.

Our divisional headquarters was in the city of Groningen. The Irish Regiment was on the right prong of the attack toward the coast. I sent out a map reference location for a cemetery to be used by Padres Rowland and Derwin Owew of the Westminster Regiment. I paid a visit to this small burial plot in which about 20 of our men were interred. It was in an isolated farmer's field adjoining a small farmhouse. Tearfully I watched one day while two small

Dutch girls gathered wild flowers and placed them in a tin on each soldier's grave. They realized the value of their freedom and were deeply appreciative of these young men who came so far to win it for them.

The day of victory, peace, and thanksgiving came with great jubilation. Most of us learned to sing for the first time that great "Dutch Hymn of Thanksgiving." Dave Rowland took a very active part in helping our division set up its conference and retreat centre for Canadian soldiers to gather together to share religious experiences. He was busy too in many official social activities as a representative of Canada in Dutch gatherings. As a good Presbyterian he was happy to find how close he was in most things to the Dutch Reform Church.

Bob Sneyd was taken into active service as a Baptist Chaplain with the Canadian Army in December, 1939. Early in his military career, he was attached to the R.C.C.S. in the Canadian National Exhibition Barracks and later the Fifth Field Regiment Royal Canadian Artillery, Camp Petawawa.

Padre Sneyd served in Britain with the 5 R.C.A. as one of the chaplains of 2 Division. In September, 1945 he was promoted to rank of H/Major and given the appointment of Assistant Senior Chaplain for CDN Armoured Division.

Padre Sneyd went into action in Normandy with 4 Division in July, 1944, and by November of that year was Senior Chaplain Second Canadian Infantry Division "In Action". H/Major Sneyd was transfered to Fifth Canadian Armoured Division as Senior Chaplain in April 1945 and returned home July of that year.

For ten years, ending in 1962, H. Major Sneyd served as Reserve Chaplain of Second Signal Regiment, Toronto. He became a member of The Canadian Council of Churches' Committee on Chaplain Service to the Armed Forces in 1948. Twice acted as chairman of this committee and for 15 years until 1982 as its secretary.

Remembrance / Joseph L. Wilhelm
–former Archbishop of Kingston

The most outstanding recollection of my service in the Second World War was not the two years spent under actual battle conditions, the various hardships connected with army life, the many acts of heroism and frustrations on the part of the engagements in Italy, and Northwest Europe, but the response of the Canadian soldier engaged in the struggle, and the fine impression that he (and she) made on the peoples of the countries, both enemy and friendly, where they found themselves ... The ordinary man and officer showed himself compassionate, friendly, sympathetic, and understanding for the most part, with the victims of war, even prisoners, and proved that they came from a country that only wanted to help these people.

The exceptions to the above only proved the unselfishness shown by the majority, and always inspired me with the worth of a way of life that was the result of hard work and common purpose for the good of all features that seem harder and harder to find in today's society.

On the Threat of Nuclear War

"Mankind seems hell-bent on its own destruction in so many ways, selfishness, greed, pollution, and other evils, that perhaps a nuclear holocaust is the natural final conclusion. But I still think that there is enough sanity and good-will to prevail, and hope and pray that saner minds will win out in the final analysis.

Father Wilhelm, enlisted as a Roman Catholic Chaplain with the rank of Hon. Captain, August 1940. Following ten months at camp Borden where he became Camp Chaplain (RC), he went overseas with the 1st Armoured Brigade and after two years in England accompanied the Three Rivers Regiment in the invasion of Sicily, July 1943. He was awarded the Military Cross and assumed the post of Brigade Chaplain until April 1944, when he was appointed chaplain with the 5th Canadian Army Hospital. Padre Wilhelm was next appointed Senior Chaplain (RC) with the 5th Canadian Armoured Division and remaind in this posting until the end of the Italian and northwest Europe campaign.

For many years he has been active with various militia units, being awared C.D. for lengthy service.

In January 1982, Padre Wilhelm was named Colonel Commandant of the Canadian Service (RC).

Remembrance /
General Clarence D. Wiseman O.C. LLD. D.D.

From "A Burning In My Bones"–The Autobiography of General C.D. Wiseman

One night an exceptionally large number of planes passed over, later we learned they were elements of the first 1000-bomber raid on Cologne. I recall thinking how brutal it all was, for however careful our men might be, inevitably innocent civilians would die and their homes would be demolished. That the enemy was guilty of the same conduct did not justify us in emulating his example. These depressing reflections haunted me as I sat dejectedly in my tent while the bombers droned above interminably. I wondered if ever they would stop. Then suddenly the air was enlivened by a sweet bird-song such as I had never heard before. In that tormented moment it evoked an instant response of celebration. Surely the wonder and glory of God's creation endures in spite of man's inhumanity to man. Though it was now quite dark and certainly not the usual hour when birds sing, other feathered choristers joined the solitary soloist until the whole forest, on the edge of which my tent was pitched, resounded to their matchless music. Not even the cruel cacophony in the high sky could still those lovely melodies. Mystified, I called my batman, and English lad who knew the countryside well, and asked the name of the birds. He informed me they were nightingales. As I fastened the flap of my tent to turn in for the night, I thanked God for brave nightingales who insisted on singing their songs of hope against such a background of death and destruction.

General Wiseman, as Honorary Captain, was posted as padre to the second battalion R.C.E. at Camp Borden, Ontario on August 1940. Shortly after he went with his battalion to England. He remained with the battalion until late in 1942. He was asked by The Salvation Army in Toronto to relinguish his commission as Chaplain, in order to assume responsibility for oversight of all Canadian Salvation Army War Services with Army, Navy and Air Force outside Canada. This involved supervision of services not only in Europe but also with the Air Force in India and Ceylon. Close liaison was maintained between the Chaplain Services and Auxiliary Services. Elected as the tenth General of The Salvation Army in May 1974, Wiseman led the world movement from its International Headquarters in London, England until retirement in 1977.

H/Major Stewart B. East

H/Capt. R. Seaborn gives a New Testament to one of the Canadian soldiers in his unit.

Ven. E.S. Light giving the "thumbs up" to a crew of 420 Squadron as they take off in their Liberator Bomber on a bombing mission over enemy territory. 1944 at #6 Group (RCAF) Station, Holthorpe, Yorkshire, U.K.

Col. John Weir Foote

H/Capt. D.A.Monson on a visit to the Basingstoke Burns and Neurological Hospital, accompanied by members of the Jewish Welfare Board.

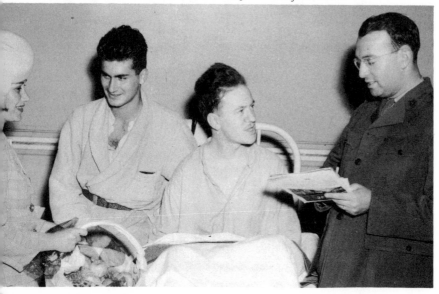

re Monson on a hospital visit in England two weeks after "V.E. Day". Others in the photo ude Anne Weinstein of the Jewish Welfare Board and patients, AC.2. Soloman Hock and LAC Bernard Clifton.

*Dr. Joseph Herman Hertz, C.H.,
Chief Rabbi of the British Empire with
Padre David Monson.*

*H/Major R.F. Sneyd in England,
1940, 5th Field Regiment
Royal Canadian Artillery.*

*Joseph L. Wilhelm,
former Archbishop of Kingston.*

*General Clarence D. Wiseman
O.C. LLD. D.D.*

Presbyterian Padres Overseas, Photographed by Mays, Aldershot. Back Row. W.S. Sutherland, R.C. Creelman, N. Sharkey, C.M. Cameron, D.C. Smith, D.B. Mackay, D.C. Hill, D.P. Rowland.

Front Row. W.D.G. Hollingworth, J.A. Munro, G.M. Jamieson, J. Logan-Vencta, G.D. Johnston, A. Mills, Wm. Sutherland, D.E. Flint.

Barry David Rowland

author and the Padre's son

born in Toronto on June 19, 1941

educated in Toronto at York Memorial Collegiate and the University of Toronto

awarded the "Bronze T" in recognition of athletic endeavours as a member of the University of Toronto Blues Football and Hockey Teams

graduated from the Faculty of Physical and Health Education in 1962

following graduation continued athletic endeavours with brief stints in the Canadian Football League and the Continental Football League

represented Canada in International Rugger in 1963

began teaching career in 1963 at former high school, York Memorial Collegiate

appointed Department Head in 1967; vice-principal in 1974

presently principal at Frank Oke Secondary School, Toronto; Provincial Director Ontario Secondary School Headmasters' Council

married; his wife Barbara and three children David, Krista and Brian reside in the Borough of York, Toronto.

Recommended Reading

Six War Years 1939-1945: Memories of
Canadians at home and abroad. *Barry Broadfoot   Doubleday, 1974*

Alex Colville: Diary of a War Artist
Alex Colville, Compiled by Graham Metson and Cheryl Lean   Numbus, 1981

A Time of Heroes 1941/1950
Stephen Franklin   Natural Science of Canada, 1977

Canada at War
Leslie F. Hannon   McClelland and Stewart, 1968

Forgotten Heroes
John Mellor   Methuen, 1975

The Canadians at War 1939/45 2 Vol.
Reader's Digest   Reader's Digest Association, 1969

Dileas
*A History of the 48th Highlanders of Canada 1929-1956
Published by the 48th Highlanders Assoc.*

Unsung Mission
by Father Jacques Castonguay   Institut de Pastorale

A Liberation Album
*Canadians in the Netherlands 1944-45
by David Kaufman/Michiel Horn
McGraw-Hill Ryerson*

The Regiment
by Farley Mowat   McClelland & Stewart

And No Birds Sang
by Farley Mowat   McClelland & Stewart

Dieppe, 1942: The Jubilee Disaster
Ronald Atkin, Guage, 1980

Not in Vain
Ken Bell   University of Toronto, 1973